**JOSSEY-BASS**
A Wiley Brand

T0329910

# Building Your Board

How to Attract Financially-capable Board Members and Engage Them in Fund Development

Scott C. Stevenson, Editor

WILEY

For general information on our other products and services or for technical support, please contact our Customer Care Department within the United States at (800) 762-2974, outside the United States at (317) 572-3993 or fax (317) 572-4002.

Wiley publishes in a variety of print and electronic formats and by print-on-demand. Some material included with standard print versions of this book may not be included in e-books or in print-on-demand. If this book refers to media such as a CD or DVD that is not included in the version you purchased, you may download this material at http://booksupport.wiley.com. For more information about Wiley products, visit www.wiley.com.

978-1-118-69193-9        ISBN

978-1-118-70412-7        ISBN (online)

# Building Your Board:

## How to Attract Financially-capable Board Members and Engage Them in Fund Development

Published by

**Stevenson, Inc.**

P.O. Box 4528 • Sioux City, Iowa • 51104

Phone 712.239.3010 • Fax 712.239.2166

www.stevensoninc.com

## TABLE OF CONTENTS

# TABLE OF CONTENTS

## START WITH YOUR NOMINATIONS COMMITTEE

*The process for building a financially capable and engaged board should begin with your board nominations committee. Who gets placed on that committee and the degree to which they understand the importance of their roles will be key to the future development of your board. It's critical that the members of this committee be in line with what you want to accomplish long term with your board. To be effective, this committee should meet no less than three times a year to review names, conduct research, make calls on prospective board members and report back findings.*

## Ideal Board Member Qualities

What qualities do you seek when considering new board members, especially those who can help strengthen your major gifts efforts? While there may be exceptions, here are some key characteristics to consider as you prioritize board candidates:

- Ability to get things done.
- Brings key talents to your board.
- Willingness to be involved in fund development.
- Respected by others.
- Ability to enlist and motivate.
- Follows through on projects.
- Compatible with other board members and CEO.
- Meets organization's gender, minority or other goals.
- Ability to separate policy from management issues.

- Affluent.
- Influential.
- Connections to wealth.
- Existing ties to your organization.
- Belief in your mission.
- Giving history to your nonprofit.
- Ability to attend meetings.
- Track record on other boards.

## Nominations Committee Is Key to Financially Capable Board

Although it's up to your nominations committee to assemble a financially capable board, it's up to you to first appoint and educate those nominations committee members. To help you toward that end:

1. **Be selective in who is named to nominations committee.** You needn't assign your wealthiest board members; however, persons named to the committee must agree on the importance of enlisting financially capable individuals. Choosing persons of influence who can attract the type of board member you seek helps.

2. **Clarify expectations.** Write down committee responsibilities. List as high priority: "To recruit financially capable board members."

3. **Meet regularly.** Your nominations committee should meet at least quarterly to review names of potential board members, gather background information, conduct interviews with board candidates and more.

4. **Help the committee realize its potential.** Share examples of other nonprofits whose boards set an example of generous giving. Help committee members understand that board support sets the precedent for all gifts that follow.

### Assemble a Can-do Committee

What characteristics do you seek when recruiting committee members? Finding people with a combination of these traits will produce a results-oriented committee:

✓ **Leadership** — Those who have assumed leadership positions in the past with your organization or others.

✓ **Listening skills** — Persons who have good listening skills and are willing to follow instructions.

✓ **Focus** — Those with the ability to concentrate on the task at hand.

✓ **Commitment** — Individuals who are willing to give the time and attention necessary to do the job right.

✓ **Perspective** — Persons who possess a balance between seeing the big picture and paying attention to details.

## Guide Your Board Nominations Committee's Efforts

To create the most financially capable board possible, it's critical that you guide and support the work of your board nominations committee. Their identification, selection and cultivation of board candidates should be an outcome of your attention to detail.

To do your part in directing the board nominations committee:

- Develop a clear description of nomination committee responsibilities and expectations.

- Share examples of ideal board candidates to help committee members identify best-choice candidates.

- Instruct your nominations committee to meet no less than quarterly.

- Invite them to submit names of capable persons you can research prior to next steps.

## Excuses for Avoiding Best Board Candidates

Too many charities avoid going after the most financially capable individuals as board members for the wrong reasons.

Here are four common excuses:

1. She's already on several other boards.
2. He has no connection with our agency.
3. She's gone a lot and may not show up for all of our meetings.
4. He's too much of a mover and shaker for our nonprofit. He'll say, "No."

If you want to enlist board members capable of raising the bar when it comes to giving, don't hesitate to go after and involve those who can make significant gifts.

### Board Selection Considerations

As your nominations committee considers new board member candidates, it may help to know whose terms on other nonprofit boards are coming to an end. Your timing may be perfect if someone's term on another board has concluded or is about to conclude.

## Spell Out Board Nominations Expectations

If you intend to attract financially capable individuals to your board, the role of your board's nominations committee should involve much more than a once-a-year meeting in which members bat around names of individuals they know. Expectations should be clearly spelled out, and the committee should meet quarterly to discuss candidates' qualifications and conduct interviews with them. Since a nominations committee is the product of its environment, you need to set high member standards.

Have a written committee description for the nominations committee and follow it. Here is an example of such a description:

### Nominations Committee Expectations

Your committee description should answer the following questions:

✓ Is there a minimum annual gift that board members should be expected to contribute?

✓ What level of importance should be placed on a board prospect's financial capability in the selection process?

✓ What level of importance should be placed on the prospect's propensity to give (e.g., past giving to your organization, philanthropic history to organizations other than yours)?

✓ What is the likelihood of the board candidate becoming actively engaged in various aspects of fund development — identifying, cultivating and/or soliciting other prospects?

✓ What would the candidate bring to the table were he/she to join the board — a particular area of expertise, a widely known/respected reputation, someone who is known for leadership and dedication?

## Identify and Prioritize Affluent Board Considerations

Regardless of what level your charity chooses to define a major gift, your board members should comprise a significant percentage of the major gift prospect pool. As you may know, it's not uncommon to have collective board member contributions account for as much as 30 to 60 percent of a capital campaign's lead gifts.

To help steer your board nominations committee in the right direction, take steps to ensure those being considered as board nominees have the potential for major gifts:

1. Sell your nominations committee on the importance of board affluence. Convince this group that major gifts can only be realized if board members set the pace.

2. Develop a file of affluent individuals to share with your nominations committee. Who among your existing constituency has the potential for exemplary giving? Also, look at names of those giving major gifts to other organizations.

3. Take action only on names submitted for consideration at an earlier nomination committee meeting. This method allows time for both staff and board members to conduct any background research that will shed more light on the candidates' financial capability and inclination to give.

## Create Nurture Plan for Financially Capable Board Prospects

Those nonprofits out to find the most financially capable board members are constantly reviewing names and adding to an ever-changing list of candidates. Some take it a step further by developing individual cultivation plans aimed at vying for these highly sought-after individuals.

To formulate a cultivation procedure for future board members:

1. Charge your board nominations committee with developing a 12-month cultivation plan for each candidate on your list.

2. Review names each time the committee meets to determine next steps for each candidate and discuss moves that have taken place since the last meeting.

3. Ask committee members to assume some level of involvement with cultivation responsibilities, having them select candidates with whom they have some familiarity or common interests.

> **Board Candidate Cultivation**
>
> Here are three cultivation strategies you may wish to incorporate using staff and/or a nominations committee member:
>
> ✓ Provide the board prospect with a tour of your facilities.
>
> ✓ Host a get-together with a board candidate and your CEO or board chair.
>
> ✓ Meet one-on-one to share personal testimonials about their experiences with your organization.

As cultivation progresses, you and committee members will develop a better sense of whom is most ready — and makes the best fit — to join your board.

## Empower Your Nominations Committee

A can-do nominations committee should do more than meet a few times a year to review and recommend names of prospective board members. But it can only do what you empower it to do.

Take steps to allow and encourage your nominations committee to help identify, cultivate and screen potential board members capable of elevating board support to new levels of giving.

Meet regularly to review names and discuss individuals' appropriateness as board members. Assign responsibility for gathering information and meeting with potential board members. Help your nominations committee understand their pivotal roles in building a foundation for future major gift support.

## Help Nominating Committee Choose Candidates

It's important that the chairperson of your board be highly supportive of the role of major gifts in the overall scheme of things or even better if he/she is a major donor and experienced at soliciting gifts.

That's why it's critical that you assist your board nominating committee by suggesting names of qualified candidates for the positions of board chair and vice chair.

While it is ultimately the committee's decision on whose names to recommend to the full board, your insight and advice will certainly guide the committee's decision-making process.

## Have a Procedure for Feeding the Committee the Names of Your Top Candidates

If it's important to build a board of financially-capable "movers and shakers," then it is imperative you provide your board's nominations committee with names of prospective candidates who measure up to your expectations. The more thought you put into that procedure, the more on track your nominations committee will become in the interview and selection process.

Develop a prioritization form such as the one illustrated here that you can use to evaluate names as they surface. Assign higher weights to criteria that you believe to be more important (e.g., financial capability). Be sure, however, to define criteria explicitly so everyone is interpreting them in the same way.

Once you have developed a master form that works for you, ask key staff to complete individual forms on a particular candidate. Then meet as a group to compare your opinions and agree on a collective ranking for that candidate based on your discussion. You can then share your staff's collective ranking of each particular candidate with the nominations committee next time it meets.

Your proactive approach in identifying capable board members will diminish the likelihood of your nominations committee grasping for names of unqualified contacts.

*Develop a board candidate rating form*
*to help prioritize names of those being considered.*

Content not available in this edition

*How do you go about identifying and approaching those individuals who you "might" want on your board? What should they know about your organization and your expectations of them prior to accepting or rejecting your offer? How might you test would-be board members to determine their potential and commitment to your organization? These are key questions that should be addressed during the recruitment process.*

## Board Member Profile Serves as Screening Tool, Magnet

A board profile is not only an effective screening device, it can serve as a magnet for attracting certain people to your board, says Doug Eadie, founder and president of Doug Eadie and Company (Oldsmar, FL), and author of "Meeting the Governing Challenge: Applying the High-Impact Governing Model in Your Organization."

"A board member profile evinces a seriousness about governing," says Eadie. "It is one of the elements that will make a board appear more attractive. It shows that the board cares enough to have a profile and makes prospective board members believe that serving on the board could be a great experience."

Such a profile describes the desired composition of the board — the mix of particular categories or groupings of members as well as their individual attributes and qualifications, says Eadie.

Whether your board is self-appointed or elected, a board member profile strengthens the composition of the board, he says. "When a board is self-appointed, the profile will help you know whom you're looking for and where to look. If your board is elected, you can circulate the profile to those who might be interested in serving."

A board member profile, he says, can help identify people with specific interests and skills who will bring different resources to the board and help build partnerships and relationships while ensuring that your board has a mix of gender, race, ethnicity and age.

Your search for board members may focus on people with board experience, a willingness and time to make a commitment, with a team-playing mentality, or with a capacity to give, says Eadie. "I have also observed an interesting and very positive spin-off of employing an ambitious board member profile in recruitment: enhanced pride and self-esteem among existing board members, who tend to take their governing work more seriously and to pay more attention to sharpening their own governing skills."

*Source: Doug Eadie, Founder and President, Doug Eadie & Company, Oldsmar, FL. Phone (800) 209-7652. E-mail: Doug@dougeadie.com. Website: www.dougeadie.com*

### How to Attract the Right Board Members

The most important job of the board operations committee? Making sure your board consists of members who are ready, able and willing to fully carry out the governing mission, says Doug Eadie, founder and president, Doug Eadie & Company (Oldsmar, FL), and author of "Meeting the Governing Challenge: Applying the High-Impact Governing Model in Your Organization."

Eadie says getting the right people for your board involves three steps:

1. Developing a board member profile that describes the desired composition of the board— the mix of particular categories or groupings of members as well as their individual attributes and qualifications.

2. Using the profile to identify and assess likely candidates to fill board vacancies.

3. Securing or influencing the appointment or election of the most desirable candidates.

"The first step in developing the desired profile is to determine the right mix of board members, and to do that you must ask: 'Whom must we have on our board to ensure that our organization continues to run smoothly, effectively delivering our services and products, satisfying our customers and clients and maintaining our financial health?'" he says. "The objective is to engage board members, the CEO and senior managers in consciously shaping—rather than merely inheriting—the board's composition."

Your board operations committee can use the board profile to identify likely candidates to fill board vacancies, he says. Have members brainstorm possibilities, drawing on their personal knowledge, or consult with other board members. It is also a good idea to cast a wider net by sending the profile to internal and external stakeholders and constituencies, says Eadie.

You may also wish to conduct more formal screening by interviewing people who are familiar with the board candidates. Have prospective board members fill out an application, including references, and interview both prospective candidates and their references, he says. "Since high-impact governing is heavily dependent on the particular people making up your board, taking a focused and systematic approach to filling board vacancies makes the best sense."

## Build a Board of Major Givers

Whether your organization is relatively new or has existed for some time, if you want to generate major gifts, it's important to build a board of directors — over time — able and willing to set an example for others.

When a charity has a capable board in place, it's not uncommon for the board's collective giving to amount to as much as 30 to 60 percent of a capital campaign goal.

What about those who are committed to your cause and willing to give of their time? Provide opportunities for involvement for these valued patrons, but limit board membership to those who can make meaningful financial gifts.

Recognizing that transforming a board takes time, here are some strategies to build board giving:

1. Recruit board members who know they are expected to contribute a minimum amount each year. Hint: The higher your expectations, the more interest you will receive from those most capable.
2. Put your most affluent board member in charge of assisting you in recruiting others of affluence.
3. Don't tolerate board members who fail to meet expectations. Ask them to step down. It's as simple as that.
4. Ask your model board donors to challenge the rest of the board.
5. Publicize exemplary board gifts as much as you can. Not only will you be cultivating the donor toward the realization of another even larger gift, you will also be encouraging other board members to follow suit.

You can't generate major gifts from board members unless you expect them.

## Be Up-front About Fundraising When Recruiting Board Members

If you want a board that plays an active role in fundraising, you must be up-front about your organization's expectations with regard to fundraising during the board recruitment process, says Jean Block, president, Jean Block Consulting, Inc. (Albuquerque, NM) and author of "Fast Fundraising Facts for Fame and Fortune."

"It's unfair not to be honest up-front," Block says. "If you blur your expectations about fundraising, assuming that when it comes to making the ask they'll be on board about it, they won't. And some will even dig in their heels."

Board members should also be expected to advocate on the organization's behalf to people in their respective circles and make an annual contribution themselves, she says.

The fundraising expert shares eight ways to involve board members in fundraising:

1. **Assist with annual and direct mail campaigns.** Ask board members to provide testimonials for your fundraising letters, write personal appeal letters to names in their contact list, make thank-you calls on donors, make fundraising calls on donors and prospects, host an event at their home or office or underwrite the campaign's cost.
2. **Get involved in your major gifts campaign.** Encourage board members to be aware of what's going on in the community, share what they learn about prospective major donors, assist in awareness, and provide outreach, underwriting, sponsorships and in-kind gifts.
3. **Secure grants from foundations and corporations.** Ask board members to research their own company's giving programs as well as other companies' giving programs. They can also provide testimonials and sign cover letters.
4. **Start a giving club.** Ask board members to set one up, name it, make the lead gift and recruit others to join.
5. **Participate in special events.** Ask board members to plan, organize or serve on special events committees and/or sell tickets and solicit auction items.
6. **Make a personal planned gift.** Ask board members to help you with planned giving efforts by serving on a planned giving committee and soliciting planned gifts.
7. **Become an advocate.** Ask board members to contact lawmakers, testify and advocate on behalf of your organization's mission.
8. **Develop a social enterprise.** Encourage board members to lead your organization in developing an earned income venture (www.socialenterpriseventures.com).

*Source: Jean Block, President, Jean Block Consulting, Inc., Albuquerque, NM. Phone (505) 899-1520. E-mail: jean@jblockinc.com*

## Groom a Board Member Recruiter

If your board could use some beefing up — based on capacity to give — why not assign that duty to one existing board member who can make a long-term difference?

Meet with your best recruiter choice and explain that, over the next three years, you intend to add new board members who have the capacity to make major gifts. (Share with the recruiter the gift range you have in mind.)

Ask the board member to help identify, research and cultivate relationships with persons who fit your criteria for board members. Meet monthly or quarterly with the board member to review names and map out plans to introduce your organization to would-be board members. Once you and the board member feel right about a particular prospect, feed that person's name to your board nominating committee for consideration.

## Groom Potential Board Members to Raise Funds Starting at Recruitment

Content not available in this edition

Providing potential board members with clear expectations about fundraising when you are recruiting them is crucial to developing a board that is comfortable with and successful at fundraising, says Jean Block, author of "The ABC's of Building Better Boards" and principal of Jean Block Consulting, Inc. (Albuquerque, NM).

"If board members are not recruited and told expressly that fundraising is a part of their key responsibilities, why are we surprised when they balk at it?" the consultant says. "Too many nonprofits are so desperate for board members that they mumble about expectations for time, talent and treasure, they aren't specific about expectations, and then just hope the new board member will eventually get it."

Instead of using this bait and switch approach which ultimately leads to feelings of resentment by board members as they come to understand expectations for fundraising, Block says nominating committees must be honest, open and clear about their expectations for board members in the recruitment phase.

To present fundraising in a way that will get buy-in from the board, she advises:

- Emphasize the importance of the mission and the purpose of the organization.
- Present the realities of the organization's fiscal position.
- Discuss plainly, and up front, that fundraising is a key responsibility of each board member. "If the prospective board member isn't willing or able to fundraise, offer him or her another avenue to support the organization," she says.
- Lead by example. "How can an organization write grants, ask for donations, etc., if their own board has not set the example?" she says. "It just isn't ethical."

To ensure board members follow through with fundraising responsibilities, Block advises using an annual commitment letter, such as the one shown below, that specifically asks for a written commitment of the person's time, talent and treasure. In addition, consider offering a specific list of ways the board members can raise funds, such as the list Block shares at left.

"I also use a Board Give and Get Form to ensure accountability. If the Commitment Letter and Give and Get Form are not returned, then the board president meets with the board member to discuss other ways to support the organization's mission," she says, adding: "You need to sometimes start with baby steps, recognize and reward accomplishments and celebrate even small successes."

*Source: Jean Block, Principal, Jean Block Consulting Inc. & Social Enterprise Ventures LLC, Albuquerque, NM. Phone (505) 899-1520. E-mail: jean@jblockinc.com*

Content not available in this edition

## Why Not Organize a Board Rush?

Are you familiar with college and university rush parties in which new students rush to get into the sorority or fraternity of their choosing? Why not use that age-old tradition as a novel way to recruit new board members? Here's how it might work:

1. **Identify ideal board members.** Identify key characteristics of those you wish to enlist as board members (e.g., capacity to give, connections to wealth, reputation).

2. **Invite existing board members to help enlist prospective board members.** Ask your board members to submit names of individuals who fit your criteria.

3. **Host a board rush reception.** Extend an invitation to identified board candidates to attend a reception hosted by your current board members. In addition to social time, share information about your organization and the role of your board.

4. **Conduct follow-up calls.** Following the event, visit one-on-one with each attendee to describe board requirements in more detail and invite them to join your board.

## Advisory Group Serves As Board Stepping Stone

Challenged by trying to recruit financially capable and dedicated board members? Why not introduce a special advisory group with an exclusive name, made up of involved individuals who can be considered for future board openings?

By having an active advisory group as an unspoken prerequisite for trusteeship, you can involve and nurture individuals who can then be considered as viable board candidates.

1. Require that board members nominate individuals to be considered for inclusion in the group.

2. Develop a job description for the advisory group members that may include responsibilities such as: regularly identifying, cultivating and/or soliciting prospects and stewarding existing donors.

3. Provide a level of cachet that makes nominees want to be a part of this exclusive group of volunteers (e.g., recognition, social opportunities and more).

## Help Board Members Recruit Others of Means

When it comes to major gifts, your board members should set the benchmark. To collectively do that, they may need to attract others of means to their ranks. You can make them more aware of that recruitment responsibility and help them in that process by:

1. Clearly stating recruitment as a board responsibility in their position description: "To identify potential board members, nurture relationships and assist in recruiting those who have the capacity to give generously."

2. Asking each board member to share the names of five individuals he or she plans to cultivate as potential board members throughout the next several months.

3. Regularly reviewing a list of financially capable individuals board members can agree to help cultivate.

4. Sharing examples of other nonprofit boards whose financial makeup reflects the level of influence you would hope to achieve.

5. Influencing who gets appointed to the board nominations committee to help ensure key steps are followed in the nomination of future board members.

## Board Recruitment Tips

✓ Convince your board to adopt an expectation policy for board giving to share with prospective board members during the interview process.

✓ To achieve the best fit when recruiting new board members, go one step beyond the traditional interview: Have the prospective board member meet with one or two current board members who can then ask questions and share their experiences and perceptions as board members.

✓ Some of the best board members are those who have past experience serving on other nonprofits' boards. That's why you should pay attention to expiring terms of those who have been involved with other groups in your community.

## INTERVIEWING PROSPECTIVE BOARD MEMBERS

*Is there a best way for approaching your top choices for board members — to avoid rejection? Just how honest should you be about expectations? Should prospective board members be formally interviewed? And once the prospective board member has accepted your offer, should there be any sort of formal agreement with your organization? This chapter will provide answers to those key questions.*

### Approach, Enlist New Board Members Judiciously

Is your board, for the most part, highly financially capable? If you launched a capital campaign, would your board members' gifts be among the largest? Would gifts of current and former board members collectively account for at least 30 percent of your campaign goal?

To recruit the most financially capable individuals, and those with the greatest likelihood of investing time and money, take your time. Don't rush it. Rather than identifying who has the most money and rushing to them with an invitation to join your board, think through your approach. To do that:

1. Conduct an interview that describes what your organization is all about and spells out board expectations in specific terms. It makes sense to have your board chair (or nominations committee chair) present to describe board responsibilities. If you're anticipating a capital campaign at some point that will require major investments of both time and resources, make your candidate aware of that possibility.

2. Insist that the interviewee take some time to think through expectations before making a final decision. You might even offer to do a facilities tour or have the individual meet with some other board members so he/she is as fully aware as possible of what's involved.

Once some time has elapsed, arrange another meeting to discuss the appropriateness of the individual joining your board. After all, new board members can either raise the bar for others or pull everyone's expectations down to an unacceptable level.

---

### What to Share With Would-be Board Members

- When interviewing potential board members, take a moment to share a list of major gifts (without names) from current and past board members — to illustrate the level of support your organization has enjoyed from this key support group.

### Clarify Board Expectations

Make it clear to board members and those being interviewed as potential board members that you expect them to assume some degree of involvement in fund development. Cite examples. Consider distributing a form they can fill out and sign that lists projects with which they agree to assist.

---

### Interview Tips for Prospective Board Members

- When interviewing a prospective board member, include another exemplary board member who can cover key expectations — level of annual giving, attendance at meetings and so forth. Neither the interviewee nor the nonprofit wants any surprises.

### Be Honest About Board Giving Requirements

If you want to recruit board members who will make personal gifts, be honest with them when discussing your board giving requirement.

If they say, "I can give you my time in service, but not money," respond with: "I appreciate that, but right now I need to take this organization to the next level, and that will require the board's financial support.'"

Then spell out expectations for board member giving, as well as to what level you expect board members to ask others for gifts.

## Interview Procedure Streamlines Board Recruitment Process

Years ago, board recruitment at North Carolina Women United (NCWU), Raleigh, NC, was an unstructured process, says Veronica Butcher, immediate past president.

"Sometimes candidates would be asked for a resume, sometimes not. Sometimes they'd be asked for biographical information, sometimes not," Butcher says. "As we grew, we realized that we really needed a more formalized process."

In addition to a new recruitment prospectus and more comprehensive application system, the process that emerged features a structured interview procedure based around standard interview questions (see below). Butcher says the new process allows them to compare the strengths and weaknesses of prospective candidates much more effectively.

The recruitment process begins with solicitations to member organizations for board member nominations. Once nominations and application forms are received, members of NCWU's governance committee interview the applicants. Interviews are conducted one-on-one, and each candidate meets with one of the five committee members. The committee then reconvenes to talk through each applicant's answers, resume and application information, and chooses the slate of candidates to bring before the general membership.

Butcher says the upgraded procedures have many benefits, not the least of which is less board turnover. "(The improved process) has helped the governance committee better articulate what we are looking for in board members, and helped candidates better appreciate what service on the board really means."

The greatest advantage of the new process, in Butcher's opinion? "Time. Formalizing your recruitment process saves so much time. For that reason alone I recommend it."

*Source: Veronica Butcher, Immediate Past President, North Carolina Women United, Raleigh, NC. Phone (866) 518-7657. E-mail: Veronica@Ncconservationnetwork.org*

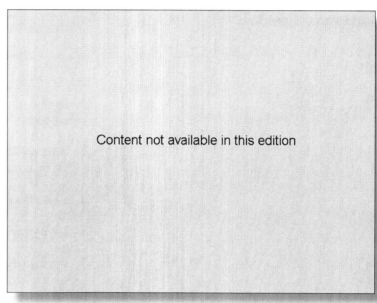

Content not available in this edition

## What to Include In Board Member Application Form

Requiring a prospective board member to fill out an application is an important part of the board recruitment process. Board candidates who take the time to fill out the form show their commitment to the organization. An application also shows prospective board members that you are serious about choosing board members.

Here are questions to consider for your board member application form:

- Why do you want to be considered for a position on our board?

- What qualifications and experience do you bring to the position?

- What is your specific interest in our organization? What do you hope to get out of your board position? (You could get these answers through a series of open-ended questions.)

- What is your volunteer experience with our organization and/or others?

- What would you like to see improved at our organization?

- What do you see as this organization's greatest strengths? Weaknesses? Biggest challenges?

- Do you feel prepared to commit the time necessary for the position?

## Make Your Board Member's Commitment Official

To demonstrate your board member's commitment to become involved in fund development on behalf of the organization he/she will represent, have him/her sign a letter of agreement similar to the example shown. In doing so, your board member agrees to support this important responsibility. The agreement also helps to eliminate any possible confusion over the roles and responsibilities of being a board member by making expectations clear.

---

### Board Member
### Letter of Agreement

I accept the invitation to become actively involved in this worthy organization in the following ways:

_____

_____

_____

_____

❑   I will do my best to set an example of generous financial support.

❑   I will participate in orientation and/or training programs to the best of my ability.

❑   I will attend regular meetings during the course of the year.

❑   I will complete assignments in a timely manner.

❑   I will do all I can to assist in generating needed resources for this organization and those served by it.

❑   Beyond my specified duties, I pledge to serve as an ambassador for this organization, speaking on its behalf to those with whom I come in contact and representing its mission with enthusiasm.

_____    _____
BOARD MEMBER                          CHIEF EXECUTIVE OFFICER


_____    _____
DATE                                         DATE

---

*Building Your Board: How to Attract Financially-Capable Board Members and Engage Them in Fund Development.* Edited by Scott C. Stevenson. © 2010 Stevenson, Inc. Published 2010 by Stevenson, Inc.

## Building Your Board

*Although board training and education should be an ongoing process, a thorough orientation will help new board members hit the ground running. There's nothing more frustrating to a new board member than to attend a year's worth of meetings and be forced to piece information together that could have just as easily been shared early in the relationship. Even if you have an existing orientation procedure in place, make time to evaluate it and examine how it might be improved upon.*

## Develop a Welcome Kit for New Board Members

Do you offer a welcome kit to new board members? Having a packet of information available for those just beginning as board members will help them get a good start. Here are some suggested items to include in the welcome kit:

- List of all board members along with their addresses and phone numbers.
- Letters of welcome from the board chairman and executive director.
- Strategic plan.
- The current budget.
- Position description that includes expectations.
- Minutes of board meetings for the past 12 months.
- Bylaws and governing documents for the board.

## Essential Elements of a Board Member Job Description

A well-written job description for your board members has many benefits. It spells out board responsibilities, makes the organization's expectations for each board member clear, and encourages accountability.

While the actual content of each organization's board job description will vary, all board job descriptions should include the following elements:

- A position summary, job title or function of the board — a brief statement outlining what each board member does, what the organization does and the general responsibilities and authorities of the board.
- Methods that will be used to evaluate board member performance.
- A confidentiality/conflict of interest statement.
- A list of the specific responsibilities of the board (including administrative, financial, time commitment and travel responsibilities).
- Term of office.
- Qualifications for becoming a board member.
- The benefits of serving on the board.
- Approval and renewal dates of the board job description.

### Examples of Board Member Job Descriptions

**Center for Independent Living for Western Wisconsin, Inc.:**
www.cilww.com/board_member_job_description.htm

**Providence Public Schools:**
www.providenceri.com/education/School_Board_Job_Description.pdf

**Iowa State University Alumni Association:**
www.isualum.org/en/about_us/isuaa_board_of_directors/board_job_description

**Santa Cruz Mountains Art Center:**
www.mountainartcenter.org/documents/Job-Descriptions/BoardMemberJobDescript.pdf

## Structure Purpose Into Board's Vice Chair Position

Too many organizations elect a vice chair without expecting him/her to do anything more than fill in when the chairperson is unable to attend a meeting.

But doing so is a big waste of talent and resources.

Why not assign special duties that allow your vice chair to accomplish some special fund development projects and prepare him/her for eventually assuming the chairperson's role?

Need some examples? Consider assigning your vice chairperson to:

1. Head up your development committee.
2. Lead the effort to focus on stewarding and expanding the number of annual $1,000-and-above donors.
3. Mobilize a campaign to raise funds for a special restricted-gift project.
4. Chair an event that reaches out to new donors.
5. Host a series of prospect rating and screening sessions throughout your community or region.
6. Oversee an annual awards program that selects recipients based on various achievement categories.

## Board Recruitment Packet Clarifies Roles and Responsibilities

Serving on the board of a nonprofit organization is an exciting prospect, but many people have a limited understanding of the responsibilities it entails, says Lee Ann Kim, founding executive director, San Diego Asian Film Foundation (SDAFF), San Diego, CA.

To help clarify those roles and responsibilities, Kim and SDAFF staff send a 12-page recruitment packet to all potential board members.

The packet "saves so much time," Kim says. "Some people receive the packet and never contact us again. But others do their due diligence and really familiarize themselves with the materials before submitting an application. Either way, the process runs much more smoothly."

The packet covers a range of topics including the foundation's vision and history, ongoing programs, staff and board member profiles, board responsibilities and committee structure, and an overview of the application process.

Board members' fundraising responsibilities are prominently featured in the foundation's explicit give or get policy. And rather than worry sharing such obligations could alienate potential board members, Kim says she believes clearly articulating financial expectations is key to building an effective board.

"Board members are responsible for ensuring organizational resources, and financial resources are a big part of that," she says. "Almost all high-functioning nonprofits have some sort of give-or-get policy. Effective boards simply need a solid base of financially capable, business-savvy members."

But while fundraising cannot be neglected, Kim says

Content not available in this edition

candidates unable or unwilling to meet such responsibilities need not be turned away. At SDAFF, she says, such persons are invited to serve on committees, assist with special events or volunteer in other ways.

"We are always looking for any and all of the three w's of work, wealth and wisdom," she says. "Financial resources are important, but there are other ways to support an organization, and you never want to turn away anyone willing to help."

*Source: Lee Ann Kim, Executive Director, San Diego Asian Film Foundation, San Diego, CA. Phone (858) 565-1264. E-mail: Leeann@sdaff.org. Website: www.sdaff.org*

## Include Board Spouses in Orientation

Even when the idea of a major gift originates with one partner of a married couple, there's no denying that the other member of the team will have a positive or negative influence on the spouse's final gift decision. In fact, in the majority of cases, major gifts from married couples are the result of a two-person decision.

That's why more nonprofits should take steps to include spouses in board orientation activities. While it may not be necessary to provide the same degree of indoctrination to board members' spouses, including and educating them will serve to cultivate their interest in your organization and make them more likely to look favorably at a future request for gift support.

While board members are experiencing orientation procedures at your organization, consider inviting spouses to take part in these types of activities:

1. Provide a tour of your facilities, pointing out services

you are able to provide because of facilities and equipment, as well as challenges posed by lack of funds.

2. Engage them in the lives of those you serve: If you represent an educational institution, for instance, let them sit in on a class for a few minutes or visit with some students. If you are associated with a medical facility, introduce them to a handful of willing patients who can talk about their experiences there.

3. If several of the spouses are from communities that are rather far away, consider providing an escorted tour of your city, emphasizing any connections to your organization's presence in the community.

4. Invite one of your accomplished employees to give a presentation or demonstration to the group on some aspect of his/her work there.

## Ask Board Members to Commit to Fund Development Duties

If you fail to communicate expectations of board members to those board members, don't be surprised when they fail to meet those expectations.

To get board members to commit to helping your fundraising efforts, offer them a choice of three or four fund development options from which they can select. Then get them to commit to those choices.

At the start of a fiscal year or whenever a new board member signs on, share a fund development menu such as the example shown here. Explain what each involvement opportunity involves and then ask the board members to sign a commitment to follow through on whatever they chose.

As you prepare your menu of choices, you will need to decide what matters most: soliciting annual fund gifts, taking a leadership role in planning a special event, helping to identify and cultivate major and planned gifts, etc.

Content not available in this edition

## Make Board Members Major Gift Sensitive

Are your board members sufficiently tuned into major gifts? If not, take steps to bring them up to speed on the importance of identifying and cultivating persons capable of making significant gifts.

It's not enough that your board members recognize the need for major gifts. They need to become sensitive to and engaged in the development of such gifts.

To help accomplish this:

1. Meet one-on-one with board members periodically to identify major gift prospects and discuss cultivation/ solicitation strategies.

2. Devote a portion of each regularly scheduled board meeting to reporting on some aspect of major gifts developments, acknowledging specific instances in which board members have been involved.

3. Regularly nurture and involve your board's development committee in major gifts development. Clearly delineate major gift responsibilities in the committee's job description.

4. Don't shy away from showing board members real-life examples of how other charities' boards take active roles in the major gifts process.

## Expose New Board Members to Inspirational Donors

To nurture new board members' interest in fund development, allow them to hear from your more generous donors.

Invite a handful of existing (non-board) donors to meet with the new board members and share testimonials about why they give and what their giving has brought to their lives.

Exposing these two groups to one another has a dual benefit: 1) board members get energized by the power of philanthropy and 2) those donors offering testimonials get even more engaged in the life of your organization and its mission.

## Learn What It Takes to Inspire Board Members

Your board of trustees needs to back a major gifts program completely and enthusiastically. After all, board members should be setting the example and raising the bar for others who will one day invest significantly in your cause.

That's why it's extremely important that board members become inspired about what major gifts can and will do for your organization. For some ideas on ways to energize them, methodically use these and other approaches:

1. Invite someone who has made a major gift — to your charity or another charity — to speak to your board.
2. Conduct an exercise in which board members discuss how they would utilize a $5 million gift if it were given to your charity. Then, after hearing and recording their dreams invite the board to spend some time discussing

what it would take to secure $5 million.

3. Invite the CEO and/or board chair of another nonprofit — with a solid history of major gifts — to meet with your board and talk about how large gifts have impacted their organization and those it serves.
4. Develop a list of institutions to which you aspire — those with significant endowments, new and enhanced facilities and equipment and programs considered cutting edge. Share the comparative list at each board meeting to demonstrate what could be realized with more major gifts.

Bringing your board members to a new level of gift expectations is a long-term process. Remain persistent in your quest to make believers of them.

## Board Training Takes Fear Out of Fundraising

Many board members lack skills to be effective, says Erin Selby, vice president, Habitat for Humanity NW Connecticut (Salisbury, CT) and a member of a number of nonprofit boards. Providing training early on can boost both their confidence and effectiveness.

"When I started volunteering for nonprofit boards, I wasn't provided with any real training or information that taught me how to be a good board member," says Selby. So when she heard of a local program called the Nonprofit Learning Center where national experts work with local boards and staff to build more effective organizations, she looked into it.

After applying Selby's organization was selected to participate in the center's six-week training session. She learned how to improve management and governance to fulfill the organization's missions more effectively through sessions on what makes an organization strong; developing an effective board; different roles of board, staff and volunteers; building and nurturing relationships that last; and strategic fund development.

In 2006, Habitat for Humanity NW Connecticut was awarded a grant by the Northwest Corner Fund (which funds the Nonprofit Learning Center class) to hire a consultant to train its 15-member board. Selby was part of the committee that chose the consultant to conduct the training. The committee used the Internet to research several consultants, and asked for referrals from Berkshire Taconic. After narrowing their choices down

to three, and interviewing each by phone, they chose Melanie Brandston from Brakeley Briscoe Inc.

"I chose (Brandston) almost immediately after beginning our phone conversation," says Selby. "Her approach in the initial conversation really snagged me. I was very impressed by her professionalism and knowledge of nonprofit boards. She was also located within driving distance, which I felt would make her a great resource for future projects."

"We worked on learning how to raise funds by personal solicitation," says Selby. "Training was very interactive. There was lots of discussion among the board members with Brandston serving as a facilitator. We learned how to manage donor objections that might come up in solicitations. We also worked on articulating and fine-tuning our mission and strategic plan as a group. The board came up with talking points to help them better communicate Habitat's mission with prospects, donors and volunteers. Melanie's approach was to take the fear out of fundraising."

The training gave the board the confidence and knowledge to go out and raise gifts, she says. "It made the board believe they could do it. My fellow board members wouldn't have said that they were comfortable about fundraising prior to this training."

*Source: Erin Selby, Vice President of the Board, Habitat for Humanity NW Connecticut, Salisbury, CT. Phone (860) 248-0405. E-mail: erinselby@snet.net*

## Involving Board Members in Fundraising Process

 ***How do you retrain existing board members to become more involved in fundraising?***

"I have often had to come into an organization and change the rules. Change is threatening and hard, but I like to see an opportunity in every situation. What I have learned over time is that if you introduce change as a mission-driven conversation, it is more likely to be accepted with an open mind, if not embraced.

"If you're going to introduce fundraising as a concept, introduce it with a deep discussion about your mission. Is it possible that as a result of this discussion you might lose some board members? Today, more funders and donors are asking if 100 percent of the board has given, and if they haven't, that will affect your ability to raise gifts."

*Source: Jean Block, President, Jean Block Consulting, Inc., Albuquerque, NM. Phone (505) 899-1520. E-mail: jean@jblocking.com*

## Ask Board Members to Sign a Board Affirmation Agreement

At the Arts & Business Council of Greater Phoenix (Phoenix, AZ), board members are asked to sign an agreement that affirms their commitment to its mission, to their legal and fiduciary responsibilities, and to the council's success.

In addition to ensuring that board members know what is expected of them, the board affirmation agreement allows the organization to release board members who are not living up to their responsibilities, says Debra Paine, executive director.

One of their board members' fiduciary responsibilities is to either give or solicit at least $2,500 a year. If, for example, a board member did not fulfill this responsibility, says Paine, the board development chair would call the board member and remind him or her.

If the board member did not fulfill the responsibility after another month, the board chair would call again and let the person off the hook by letting them leave the board.

"The board chair might say to the board member, for example," says Paine, "'We understand the financial times and that you've been unable to live up to your commitment. Maybe there will be a better time in the future when you can serve on the board. We're going to release you from your commitment.'"

*Source: Debra M. Paine, Executive Director, Arts & Business Council of Greater Phoenix, Phoenix, AZ. Phone (602) 234-4711. E-mail: dpaine@artsbusinessphoenix.org*

*This board affirmation agreement clarifies the expectations of board members at the Arts & Business Council of Greater Phoenix (Phoenix, AZ).*

Content not available in this edition

## ENGAGE YOUR BOARD IN FUND DEVELOPMENT

*Give, get or get off. Time, talent and tithing. These are long-held axioms describing key responsibilities of board members who represent nonprofit organizations. Clearly, every board member should bear some level of responsibility with regard to fund development and personal giving. You job is to engage them, both as a group and individually, in ways that maximize their contributions of time and talent and to do that in meaningful ways.*

## Get Board Buy-in for Your Operational Plan

What happens after you have spent time developing a yearlong operational plan that outlines all of your fundraising strategies for the upcoming year?

A logical next step would be to coordinate a retreat for your board (or board development committee) to share goals and ask for their input.

Here's one way to do that:

1. Arrange a day-long planning session in a casual setting.
2. Have members of your development team share goals, objectives and strategies with those present. Clarify that the plan is a first draft and will be finalized following their input.
3. Identify key areas throughout the plan that require and welcome board involvement. Give those present the opportunity to decide how they can help address objectives by expanding on existing strategies or developing entirely new strategies for which they are responsible.

Your board's involvement in planning will ensure ownership for achieving goals.

## Invest Board Members in Development Planning

You know that development planning leads directly to dollars raised, which supports the very existence of your organization. But how do you educate board members to make sure they feel the same way?

The following tips can help:

✓ **Include a specific developmental planning component.** Of course you need to revisit the current strategic plan and reassess the vision, mission and goals included at your next planning retreat. But try and set aside some time for education on a specific issue of development (e.g., planned giving, board committee development, etc.) This will allow your members to focus on one area of the plan and give them a better understanding of the work involved and where they can help.

✓ **Make sure the end product is an active plan.** In spite of best intentions, sometimes planning is the beginning and the end of the development process. Make sure your board knows that the plan will be put into action with specific, measurable steps in a timely manner. Share specific examples of how the planning process has been successful in the past.

✓ **Engage persons with experience.** If you are fortunate enough to have someone on your board with prior fundraising experience, actively involve that person in spearheading the planning process. He/she will add credence to the importance of the retreat and the process, as well as professional insight. Just make sure they work with your facilitator in advance so they're not stepping on any toes.

*Sources: Michael Alstad, Executive Director, Music Center of the Northwest, Seattle, WA. Phone (206) 526-8443.
E-mail: malstd@mcnw.org
Dawn Welch, Asante Health System, Medford, OR.
Phone (541) 472-7301. E-mail: Dwelch@asante.org*

## Ask Board Members, Others to Help Identify Prospects

How often are you asking board members, close friends of your organization and employees to share names of major gift prospects?

It's good stewardship to ask for referrals on at least a quarterly basis. Asking for referrals not only produces new names, it impresses upon those you ask how important major gifts are to your organization's future.

By asking for others' help and input, you're influencing them to become more committed to your major gifts program.

Regularly make a point to:

✓ Ask board members at each regular meeting to write down names of persons they know who are capable of making a $25,000-or-larger gift to your organization.

✓ Ask employees, either in group meetings or one-on-one, to share names of potential donors they know or suspect to be worth additional research.

✓ Never leave a donor who has just made a gift commitment without asking for the name of one or two other individuals he/she knows who might be capable of a similar gift.

## ENGAGE YOUR BOARD IN FUND DEVELOPMENT

### Ask Every Board Member to Help You Network

To make new contacts with persons of wealth, be proactive in asking board members to include you in get-togethers with their friends and associates. Your simple presence could open doors leading to further meetings.

Extend an invitation for board members to think how they might include you as a friend in group get-togethers. Share some examples of how that might occur:

- Joining them as a guest at some other nonprofit's fundraiser.

- Accompanying them to a Chamber of Commerce event.
- Inviting you to join a foursome in a round of golf.
- Inclusion on their guest list for private dinner parties and receptions.
- Accompanying them to civic club meetings.
- Introductions to their company's top decision makers.

In addition, encourage board members to ask their spouses to include you in group gatherings if and when appropriate.

### Engage Wealthy, Powerful Board Members With Discretion

The perfect board member: one who holds a powerful and visible position, has several ties to others with wealth, is financially capable and willing to give generously.

Whenever you are fortunate enough to have a person of such stature on your board, make the most of engaging him/her in reaching out to others, but be judicious in how you approach using the person's time so as not to risk alienation.

To help prioritize the ways in which you can involve a more powerful board member, and also allow him/her to have some say in the process, share an opportunities-for-involvement list tailored to that individual. That way, when you first meet with the board member, you can review those opportunities, sharing projects you deem most important and allowing the board member to see the big picture. This gives the board member some sense of how he/she might best allot available time and avoid being surprised and annoyed at repeated requests for assistance.

Your tailored opportunities for involvement will vary from board member to board member. For some, the list may be oriented toward approaching other individuals for introduction, cultivation and solicitation purposes. For others, your goal may be to share leadership opportunities (e.g., serving as steering committee chair or heading up your annual community campaign). Producing the list forces you to identify how to best make use of a board member's limited time and helps that board member better visualize the full scope of available opportunities.

---

Opportunities for Involvement
Prepared Especially for

**John Doe, CEO, XYZ Corporation**

**Introductions and cultivation of key prospects** — This would involve discussing how we can best introduce our organization to these individuals with your help and then developing cultivation plans for each, leading to their eventual solicitation.

_____ Alfred Docker, CEO, Alfred Docker Foundation

_____ Mary and Tom Beckwith, FASKMO Industries

_____ Frank Weinstein

_____ Marty and Kathryn Walsh

**Prospect solicitation** — Although the following individuals are familiar with our organization, your presence and involvement in their solicitation would help greatly in maximizing their contribution.

_____ Alex M. Fraizer, CEO, Fraizer, Inc.

_____ Elizabeth E. Beckmann, Owner, A-1 Moving and Storage

_____ Walter Z. Metterhorn, President, 1st Central Bank

_____ D. L. Christiansen, Owner, Triad Packaging, Inc.

_____ Jack Hartman, Chairman, Hartman Building Supply

**Letter-signing appeal** — We would like you to consider signing a letter to approximately 50 key individuals, inviting their generous support of our annual fund by becoming members of the Founder's Society (gifts of $1,000 or more). An invitation coming from you, on your letterhead, would carry significant weight in influencing their decision to join the Founder's Society. This appeal would be signed in February. Personal notes on each letter would be appreciated but not necessary.

## Leverage the Powerful Reputations of Your Board Members

Board members articulate strategic direction, provide organizational continuity and often supply their share of elbow grease to a nonprofit's mission. But beyond the services they provide, their reputation in the local, regional or national community can be of great benefit as well.

Larry Stybel understands how boards operate inside and out. He is co-founder and vice president of Board Options, Inc. (Boston, MA) — a nationally recognized company specializing in helping boards be effective problem-solving units through the application of practical behavioral science — and executive in residence at the Sawyer School of Business at Suffolk University (Boston, MA).

Here, Stybel shares his expertise in the art of leveraging the reputation of prestigious board members:

### What is the central rationale behind showcasing well-known board members?

"Donors, when they were children, were told by their mothers that they would be known by the company they keep. This is what board members do for nonprofits. If you are an up-and-coming nonprofit that does not have top-flight status, one way to create reputation and cache is through your board members. In branded institutions like MIT or Princeton, the institution gives luster to the board member. But in smaller organizations, the opposite is true: board members lend their credibility to the nonprofit."

### So in attracting donors and other prospective board members...

"Prestigious board members function like the anchor store of a shopping center, the place that all the other shops cluster around. If a brand-name person is on your board, other people will want to be associated with that individual, and, by extension, your organization and its mission."

### Are there any challenges to having well-known board members?

"If you are not a prestigious institution, there is a limit to how many brand-name people you can afford to have on your board. Two is great; six might not be so great. One of the disadvantages of bright star board members is that they often have only limited time to put into your organization. They will not typically be the 'shirtsleeves' board members who dig in and really get things done. Bright stars are important, but they are prone to fighting with each other, and too many can be counterproductive."

> ### Profit From Board Members' Connections
>
> Do you have any powerful board members who serve on various corporate boards? Don't overlook the fact that those corporate connections may represent matching gift companies that will match your board member's gifts.

### What should organizations know about using the name of a bright star board member?

"That it should always be done with the knowledge and agreement of the board member. That individual is lending his or her name and stature to your organization, and you don't want to abuse that privilege. A bright star should never find out you used his name after the fact. And also be aware that if he is a CEO or president, his business will often want to clear the use of the name beforehand as well."

### Is there anything a shirtsleeves-heavy board should do or not do in looking for bright star members?

"One tip is to make board participation a finite commitment. Prestigious individuals don't want to be trapped on the board of a smaller nonprofit forever, even if they believe in its mission. Setting a term limit of two or three years spares them the awkwardness of resigning and makes them more likely to agree to the initial commitment."

*Source: Larry Stybel, Co-Founder and Vice President, Board Options, Inc., Boston, MA. Phone (617) 594-7627. E-mail: Lstybel@boardoptions.com*

## Teach Board Members to Nurture Relationships

Board members can play a powerful role in making introductions and cultivating relationships on your organization's behalf.

To make them more aware of their potential and encourage them to assume a more proactive role in making introductions with and cultivating major gift prospects, follow these steps:

1. Regularly share lists of nondonor prospects with board members. Ask them to select names of individuals, businesses and/or foundations they are willing to cultivate in various ways.
2. Share examples of board members or other volunteers who took the time to introduce your charity, particularly those that eventually resulted in major gifts.
3. Make board members aware that you, or another staff person, are ready and willing to accompany board members on visits to would-be donors.
4. Encourage working in pairs if they find doing so more comfortable or productive.
5. Compliment board members who are performing and producing as expected. Do so in the presence of other board members.

## Get Your Board Engaged in Backing Planned Gifts Program

Your board's support (or lack of it) for your planned gifts program will impact its long-term success. Enthusiastic support can accelerate planned gifts tremendously. Consider these steps to strengthen your board's commitment to and involvement in marketing planned gifts:

✓ Evaluate planned giving programs of nonprofits more advanced than yours and share finding with your board to raise your board's sights.

✓ Work with your board to establish planned gift goals. Engage members in shaping challenging yet realistic goals.

✓ Involve your board in establishing and evaluating a planned gifts policy. Does your nonprofit accept charitable remainder unitrusts? Should the board OK accepting bequests that include restrictions? Addressing such ongoing questions establishes the foundation of your planned gifts program and engages board members.

✓ Set a yearly calendar of activities and events inviting board participation: estate planning seminars, recognition of planned gift donors and more.

✓ Involve board members in shaping your planned giving budget. Share an itemized budget to show what you are able to accomplish plus how additional resources could be used.

✓ Recognize board members who give time and support to your planned gifts efforts to keep them motivated and also encourage others to become more involved.

✓ Meet one-on-one with board members to seek their input and expertise. Invite board members to make referrals and help in the cultivation of likely prospects.

### Establish Planned Gift Goals

Involve your board in establishing quantifiable objectives that move your program forward in securing new planned gifts. Consider goals such as:

❑ To identify ___ planned gift prospects in the current fiscal year.

❑ To average ___ personal visits each week with planned gift prospects.

❑ To solicit a minimum of ___ planned gifts throughout the current fiscal year.

❑ To secure ___ planned gift expectancies amounting to at least $___ during the current fiscal year.

❑ To expand the planned gifts mailing list by ___ during the current year.

❑ To conduct ___ estate planning seminars during the current year.

❑ To enlist ___ centers of influence who will assist our planned gifts efforts by identifying and cultivating would-be donors.

❑ To invite all board members to consider our charity in estate plans.

✓ Invite individual board members to make planned gift commitments to your cause.

✓ Keep board members abreast of information affecting the world of planned giving: issues being addressed at the national level, demographics and more.

## Involve Board Members in Your Special Events

Whether you're coordinating a walk, a black-tie gala or a chili cook-off championship, there's value in getting board members involved in your special events.

Although other volunteers may be heavily committed to planning and executing an event, be sure your board has some degree of responsibility for carrying off a successful fundraiser. Ask members, for instance, to each be responsible for selling a minimum number of tickets or enlisting sponsors.

Most importantly, convey the importance of their presence at your event. Provide them with distinctive badges that separate them from all others.

Board attendance at special events:

• Helps to strengthen board ownership of the organization.

• Gives board members a better understanding of how such events fit into the overall development plan.

• Provides board members the opportunity to act as ambassadors on behalf of the agency.

• Allows your board to experience a more festive aspect of their association with your organization.

## A Prominent Board Does More Than Give

The composition of your board will play a key role in your ability to attract major gifts. For starters, during a capital campaign, board gifts can account for as much as 30 percent or more of the campaign goal. In addition to your board's financial capability:

1. **The collective reputation of your board can elevate your charity's standing in the minds of major gift prospects.** For example, when a prospect receives a letter from your organization that has several recognizable and prominent names listed as board members, your organization's credibility is heightened.

2. **Board members can open doors to others who possess wealth.** Whether they host receptions for friends, accompany you on a call to one of their associates or sign a letter on behalf of your organization, reputable board members will amplify your ability to make new major gift connections.

## Prepare Board Members, Volunteers for Team Solicitations

Before asking board members or other volunteers to participate in donor solicitation calls, know the roles everyone will play, says Marion Conway, principal, Marion Conway Consulting (Verona, NJ).

"Does the board member/volunteer represent the link to the potential donor as a friend, business associate or alumni of the same college, or does he or she represent an added representative from the organization?" Conway says. "Their role may be different depending on their relationship with the potential donor."

In either case, board members/volunteers should share with the prospect their connection with the organization and passion for its mission, their personal relationship with its work and events, how it benefits their family and the community.

Discussing major goals of the strategic plan and the vision for the organization's future is also valuable and appropriate, Conway says.

Meet in advance of the solicitation call to discuss these roles so there are no surprises at the call, she says. Cover the type of questions they will answer, and which questions you will handle: "For example, if you have developed a list of program options that the donor might support, the board member or volunteer may help figure out which options are most likely to appeal to the donor."

If the board member/volunteer has a personal relationship with the potential donor, it is appropriate for him or her to make the ask, says Conway, because it can be done in an informal and personal way. "If the board member/volunteer does not have a personal relationship with the donor, it is better for you to make the ask. In either case you should know what the specific ask will be."

*Source: Marion Conway, Marion Conway Consulting, Verona, NJ. Phone (973) 239-8937. E-mail: mc@marionconwayconsulting.com. Website: marionconwaynonprofitconsultant.blogspot.com*

## Help Board Members Make Asks

When it comes to asking others for gifts, do your board members drag their feet?

Christina Thrun, development and marketing director, Big Brothers Big Sisters of Northwestern Wisconsin (Eau Claire, WI), shares a method her organization uses to get board members over their hesitation and engaged in seeking gifts: The Big Magic Breakfast, which has helped board members raise nearly $250,000 since 2004.

The event is based on the Raising More Money or Benevon Model of fundraising, which trains and coaches nonprofit organizations to implement a mission-based system for raising sustainable funding from individual donors.

For the breakfast, board members serve as table captains and fill a table of seven by inviting friends and colleagues. Staff provides them with tools and information on how to ask guests to participate, which makes it easier for them. No mass invitations are sent out for the event, which is designed to generate multiple-year gifts.

The breakfast runs 7:30 to 8:30 a.m. and includes a pro-

gram that is about 35 minutes long with speakers such as the organization's CEO and board president, a volunteer/mentor and someone involved in the school system who can speak to the organization's impact on students.

At the end of the program, table captains pass out pledge cards and the board president asks people to make a gift.

Thrun says, "This event is a bit more of a high-pressure ask, but it's not a direct ask. By doing this event, our board members don't have to visit with people one-on-one and ask them to make a gift. Many of our board members really like this event and have chosen these events over the one-on-one approach."

She says the event has also been popular among donors and invited guests. "We've received a lot of great feedback from guests, who indicate how moving the event is. We've yet to have an event with completely dry eyes."

*Source: Christina Thrun, Development and Marketing Director, Big Brothers Big Sisters Northwestern Wisconsin, Eau Claire, WI. Phone (715) 835-0161. E-mail: Christina.Thrun@bbbs.org*

## Turn Your Board Members Into Fundraisers

Want to get your board members more involved in fundraising? Just ask.

Staff with Advocates for Youth (Washington, D.C.) ask board members to complete a commitment form that outlines ways they can help raise money for the organization.

"It's important to recognize that some board members won't be comfortable fundraising, no matter what," says Elizabeth H. Merck, manager of individual giving. "The key is to figure out a way that they can get involved in fundraising that doesn't intimidate them."

The form provides about 20 options for board members to choose from, including:

❑ Serving on the fundraising committee

❑ Making phone calls to thank donors for their gifts

❑ Writing personal notes on fundraising appeal letters

❑ Sending informational packets to five people by mail and asking them to make a gift

❑ Providing the names of five individuals to add to the mailing list

❑ Providing an introduction to at least one major donor prospect

❑ Hosting an event

❑ Pledging to search the Web using GoodSearch

❑ Pledging to shop online using GiveBackAmerica.org

Merck follows up with board members throughout the year to make sure they're fulfilling their commitments.

*Source: Elizabeth H. Merck, Manager of Individual Giving, Advocates for Youth, Washington, D.C. Phone (202) 419-3420, ext. 24. E-mail: liz@advocatesforyouth.org*

## Teach Board Members Through Your Example

There is no better way to teach board members to become accomplished fundraisers than to learn by doing. To nurture them as solicitors of major gifts, build the following steps into your routine:

1. **Take individual board members on thank-you visits to existing donors.** Stewarding major donors is critical to receiving repeat gifts, and there is no better person to bring on a thank-you call than a board member. The process of calling on donors to say thanks will be an energizing experience for board members and prepare them to make asks in the future.

2. **Make learning calls on prospects in which you each have designated roles.** Begin involving individual board members in making cultivation or solicitation calls with you. Although you can assume the solicitation role, the accompanying board member can play a supporting role, answering questions about your organization and offering testimonials about the benefits of supporting it. Discuss who will cover what in advance of each call.

3. **Encourage more experienced board members to make calls with other board members.** Once board members have made sufficient calls with you (or other staff persons) to become confident in the solicitation role, encourage them to make team calls with other experienced board members.

4. **Share your own results with board members.** Allow them to learn from both your successes and failures. Offer personal examples of what you have done correctly and instances in which a change in tactics might have proven more successful.

This incremental nurturing process should be ongoing. Don't wait for a capital campaign to get under way before building a corps of accomplished board solicitors.

## Get Your Board to Assume Responsibility for Annual Gifts

It's not uncommon for boards to think it's the responsibility of staff to meet annual fund goals. That's wrong. Board members should feel some sense of ownership for meeting and exceeding annual gift goals.

Engage your board in annual giving by getting them to approve some portion of your annual giving goal. Depending on your board's size and level of past involvement, convince the board development committee to accept responsibility and seek full board approval for any of these yearly goals:

✓ To secure [X] number of gifts throughout the fiscal year within a defined gift range (e.g., $500 and above).

✓ To individually sell so many special event tickets each year (or purchase those they don't sell).

✓ To individually contribute a minimum amount to the annual fund each year.

✓ To individually make a minimum number of solicitation calls on new prospects.

## Thank-you Calling Campaign Involves, Inspires and Educates Board Members

Board members at SHALVA (Chicago, IL) — a nonprofit that provides domestic violence counseling services to the Jewish community — regularly call donors to say thanks.

"I think it is impossible to thank donors too much for supporting SHALVA's programs, especially given the current fundraising environment," says Ava Newbart, director of development. "These simple thank-you calls are a great opportunity for SHALVA to personally connect with donors. They are also a way to inspire our board to keep fundraising and promoting SHALVA to our community."

Since SHALVA's office has only four phone lines and a small budget, Newbart asks board members to call donors on their own.

For their first calling campaign, board members called all year-end donors of $50 or more. Newbart e-mailed board members a script, call report form and a list of names with phone numbers. Each board member was asked to make an average of 20 phone calls, for a total of approximately 400 calls.

Newbart followed up with board members via e-mail, encouraging them to make their calls and send her back the forms. "One board member e-mailed me back and asked, 'You want me to call, say thank-you and not ask for anything else? Are you sure?'" she says. "I reassured her, and other board members, that their phone calls would be well received and that they would be happily surprised at donors' responses."

She also reminds board members that with the economy as it is, SHALVA must reach out and personally contact donors; that it's much easier to keep current donors than to find new donors; and that the need for SHALVA's services is on the rise.

For other nonprofits considering starting a simple thank-you campaign, Newbart advises: "Just do it and keep it simple. Being a one-woman shop is challenging. We've talked about making personal thank-you calls for a long time, but there were always competing priorities. Given the climate, our board was open to trying new strategies. Keeping our donors happy is an agency-wide mantra."

*Source: Ava Newbart, Director of Development, SHALVA, Chicago, IL. Phone (773) 583-4673. E-mail: anewbart@shalvaonline.org*

*Staff with SHALVA (Chicago, IL) provide tools to board members to make donor thank-you calls. They are the call report, below, and informational sheet, at right.*

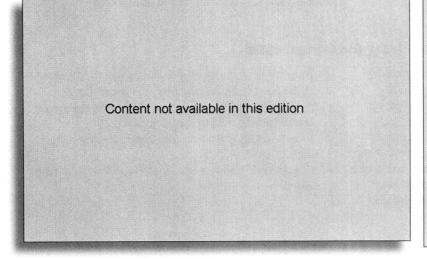
Content not available in this edition

**The Conversation:**
The intention of your call is ONLY to thank donors for their gifts received.

**Sample Opener:**
"Hello, Mr./Mrs. X. My name is Jane Brown and I'm a member of the volunteer board of directors of SHALVA. I am calling to thank you for your support of our organization. We received your recent gift and I wanted to let you know, personally, how very much we appreciate it."

At this point, simply pause and wait for a response. Some donors are quite startled and don't know what to say. Usually, they are very appreciative and gracious.

Most calls are very short, simply ending after you express your thanks. **Please do NOT make any comment that could be construed as another request,** such as "We are grateful for your gift and hope you will continue to support us in the future." This hints of another solicitation, and we want to avoid leaving that impression.

**Sample Closer:**
You can end the call by simply wishing the donor a pleasant evening.

Sometimes a caller will ask you about how SHALVA is doing or will want some information about our programs and services. If you are comfortable answering their questions, by all means do so. If not, perhaps you could ask if they would like a staff member to contact them separately. If so, please let us know. If a donor expresses an interest in giving more or in volunteering time, you can definitely engage in that discussion. Other organizations' experience with thank-you calls by board members has shown that a small number of donors want to discuss making an additional gift and sometimes it can be significantly higher than the gift they have recently made.

**What happens as a result of these calls?**
Donors who receive a personal call (including those who received messages left on answering machines) will be specially coded by the office, and any additional information gathered during the calls will also be recorded.

The next time these donors are solicited along with other donors who did not receive a call, we will be able to compare their average gift levels, their rate of response, the promptness of response and other information. We can continue to compare these groups for a couple of years, which will allow us to measure long-term loyalty of the two groups. Though we anticipate that donors who receive personal calls are likely to show greater loyalty over time and make increasingly generous gifts, we need reliable information from this test for future planning and forecasting.

## DEVELOPMENT COMMITTEE AND BOARD MEETINGS

*Whatever you choose to call it, the Board Development Committee should be closely connected to every aspect of your fundraising efforts and serve as your department's spokesperson and advocate at all regularly-scheduled board meetings. In addition, they should meet regularly outside of board meetings and assume some level of responsibility in fund development activities. Duties may include but not be limited to: reviewing names of donors/prospects, making cultivation, solicitation and/or stewardship calls, managing activities surrounding a higher-level gift club, organizing a special campaign or event and more.*

## Development Committee Is Key to Other Board Members

How seriously do your board development committee members take their roles? Do they fully realize their committee's potential in generating major gifts?

It's important that these key people recognize their principle job is to institutionalize development within the full board. That means engaging the full board in fund development and helping members to more fully understand their potential. Your development committee can help make that happen by:

✓ Conducting a self assessment or self evaluation.
✓ Inviting their colleagues to make generous annual contributions.
✓ Inviting fellow board members to set a high precedent for campaign contributions.
✓ Inviting board members to consider making planned gifts.
✓ Encouraging board members to get involved in various aspects of fund development.

## Keep Development Committee Members Up-to-date

It's nice to get a thank-you letter from a charity employee. But it's much more powerful and meaningful to receive a letter from a board member or volunteer — someone who's not getting paid to say "thank you."

Whenever your development committee meets, include current information about donors and prospects that members can act on if they choose. Whether it's a handwritten note for a recent gift or a birthday card, the added touch of these devoted individuals will only serve to strengthen your organization's ties to both donors and prospects.

Items you may wish to make development committee members aware of include:

✓ Recent contributions of previous and new donors.
✓ Upcoming special dates of donors: birthdays, anniversaries, etc.
✓ Job promotions and other news items related to donors and prospects.

Give your committee members some stationery and note cards with your organization's letterhead, so the recipient of the card or letter will make an immediate connection with your organization.

## Nurture Your Development Committee Chair

Just as it's important that you provide on going training for your development committee — whether that's a board committee or a separate group — it's equally important that you make time to train and nurture the person chairing that committee. Here are some ways to do that:

1. Review historical gift data so the chair knows who is giving and at what levels.

2. Review your most recent year's fundraising strategies (e.g., direct mail, phonathon, face-to-face calls) to help

him/her get an understanding of what's being done.

3. Share key challenges/opportunities facing your department for the current and upcoming year.

4. Present your top five ideas on ways the development committee can make a meaningful impact in supporting your department's objectives.

After following these steps, allow and invite your chairperson to help shape a plan of action.

## Have the Development Committee Chair Give Board Reports

Many nonprofit boards have a development committee. But all too often, when the board holds regular meetings, it's an employee — not a committee member — who gives the development report. That's the wrong approach. If you want an active development committee, the chair of that committee should be the one giving those reports to the full board. Your board chair will be more engaged and more committed to achieving results if he/she is responsible for bringing business to the full board.

To help your development committee chair deliver a convincing report, meet with him/her prior to each board meeting. Go over each item to be presented to the board, pointing out where he/she can refer to you to share additional details. Don't hesitate to ask your chair about particular issues to be sure he/she has a thorough understanding of each topic. Point out the "why" behind each topic to be presented: Why is this issue important to the board? Why should the board adopt this policy?

Having your development committee chair make the development report makes him/her a more committed team member while adding credibility to what's being presented.

## Share Key Information at Each Board Meeting

Use regularly scheduled board meetings to truly educate and inform the people who attend them.

Although the usual reports and policy issues serve to educate, there are certain facts board members may never learn unless you make a point to convey that information to them. And, because board members are only exposed to your organization periodically, certain facts may need to be repeated often.

Regardless of how you present this information, here are some facts all of your board members should be familiarized with over time:

- The size of your budget.
- Annual payroll.
- Number of clients (e.g., students, patients, families) served during specified periods of time.
- Size of endowment and average rate of return on investments.
- Number of employees.
- Your mission statement.
- Percent of total budget made of gift revenue.
- Significant foundation/government grants — amounts and uses.
- Benchmark statistics that position your organization's achievements.

## Use Board Meetings to Rally Enthusiasm

Don't use regularly scheduled board meetings to simply report boring gift statistics. Instead, approach them as an opportunity to build enthusiasm and support for your fundraising objectives.

Although you may meet one-on-one with individual board members from time to time, board meetings represent the single best opportunity for collectively cultivating and persuading members to buy into your plans.

Consider some of these ideas as you prepare for your next board meeting:

- Select four or five similar agencies that have achieved superior fundraising success and use them as models to build board enthusiasm.
- Invite a recent major donor (nonboard member) to attend the next meeting and tell the board what inspired him/her to make a significant gift to your cause.
- Conduct a brainstorming exercise with board members to discuss what it would take to generate a history-making gift for your organization. What would have to change in order for that to happen?
- Assemble a panel of those served by your institution (e.g. students, youth, former patients) to discuss — in the board's presence — why they think your charity is worthy of major gifts.
- Invite a foundation officer to tell board members what it takes to merit the foundation's financial support.
- Share a massive list of your community's nondonors with the board and ask them what it would take to convert a percentage of those named to donor status.

## Bring Life, Enthusiasm to Your Board Presentation

If you're responsible for providing a development report at regularly scheduled board of trustees meetings, work at bringing life to your presentation rather than going through numbers that might be perceived as the same old thing.

In addition to updating board members, your goal should be to engage them in fund development and uplift their enthusiasm in the benefits of increased gift revenue. Instead of walking through a gifts-to-date report at each meeting:

1. Point out the impact of a major gift one or two years after it was made.

2. Invite and publicly introduce any new donors who gave over a threshold amount.

3. Share a fundraising issue facing your department as you invite board input the development committee can use in forming a board recommendation.

4. Offer some recent anecdotes that point out the rewards of cultivating and soliciting donors.

5. Have two or three people attend who have benefited from annual gift support. Invite them to talk about the impact of giving on them.

## What Should You Report to Your Board and Volunteers?

Campaign progress reporting is a powerful tool for both fundraising professionals and an organization's professional staff and volunteer leadership, says Roy P. Wheeler, Jr., executive vice president, Custom Development Solutions (New York, NY).

It is important to quickly and effectively set the pace and tone for campaign communications and monitoring at the beginning of the campaign, Wheeler says. Doing so helps make the effort a success while allowing issues to be addressed early on, helping to foster the best working relationship among staff, board and volunteers.

The major gift officer or consultant is responsible for establishing immediate and clear lines of communication with top professional staff and volunteer leadership (directors or trustees), especially within current development operations, Wheeler says. "This eases accomplishment of the tasks required during the course of the campaign, and facilitates everyone's understanding of what is happening, and who is responsible for making it happen. The progress report is the primary tool in this strategy."

Wheeler establishes report cycles up front, as well as who should be reported to, then creates a first report that outlines each major campaign activity. He presents this report in a special meeting, first with the top development professional, then with the chief professional officer of the organization.

Once Wheeler has buy-in of these key persons, he schedules a meeting to present the report to his volunteer leaders.

Finally, he presents a formal copy of the report to the organization's board as an agenda item at a regular board meeting.

When making a report, Wheeler says, "You need to take into account that there will be some crossover as a campaign builds a parallel leadership team focused on the campaign, but that typically includes key board members and professional staff."

*Source: Roy P. Wheeler, Jr., Executive Vice President, Custom Development Solutions, Inc., New York, NY. Phone (800) 761-3833. E-mail: rpw@cdsfunds.com*

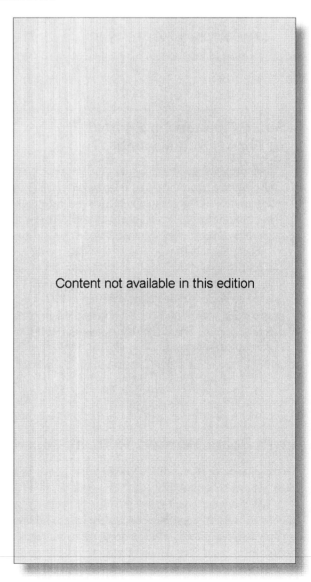

Content not available in this edition

## Nurturing Your Board

How often does your board meet? Do members travel to attend your meetings?

If your board members' time and distance prohibit them from regularly seeing your organization in action, be sure to expose them to your mission when they are in town. Whether it's before, during and/or after the meeting, plan activities that serve to inspire and energize them and provide justification for making major investments of time and financial resources. Examples of such activities might include:

✓ Interacting with those being served by your organization (e.g., students, youth, former patients).

✓ Touring particular departments, facilities or construction projects.

✓ Meeting with particular employees to learn more about their work and contributions.

## Think Through Board Report

When readying your regular development report for a board meeting, think about what you want your message to accomplish. Do more than simply share information about gifts to date.

Do you want your report to help build board ownership of fund development? Show how board gifts set a precedent for those that follow. Or perhaps you want to emphasize the value of placing greater focus on garnering gifts in the $1,000-and-above range.

By thinking about what you want your presentation to accomplish, you can accompany your development update with messages aimed at influencing board members in particular ways.

## Share Fundraising Efforts At Each Board Meeting

If your organization doesn't have much history at raising funds, be sure to provide your board with a written and oral report at all regularly scheduled board meetings. This both informs them about what's going on and helps them to own your development efforts.

Share a standard report of gifts to date for the current fiscal year, and break down the sources of those gifts (e.g., businesses, individuals, employees, etc.) in relation to goals. Additionally, summarize fundraising projects that will occur between now and the next board meeting, inviting board members to take an active role in particular aspects.

## Stress Major Gifts' Weight At Board Meetings

How do you point out the importance of major gifts during board meetings? No other audience is more important than your board members, when it comes to selling them on their importance to your charity's future. Turn their attention to major gifts by:

• Reporting on major gifts plans and progress at each meeting.

• Publicly introducing anyone who has made or played a key role in securing a significant gift since the last board meeting.

• Discussing/approving policy issues related to major gifts.

## Invite Board Members to Thank Generous Contributors

Getting a note or phone call of appreciation from a board member can be impressive.

Whether your board meets monthly or quarterly, provide them with a list of contributors since the last board meeting and invite those present to write down the names and addresses of those they would be willing to write or phone with a message of appreciation. The simple but regular exercise of having board members thank your more generous contributors helps them more fully appreciate the role of philanthropy in your ongoing operations and also helps ready them for eventual solicitation calls.

## Instruct Board Members to Introduce You and Your Cause

Do you have a method to encourage board members to introduce you and your organization to individuals, businesses and foundations?

If your board is made up of "movers and shakers," they should be in positions to help introduce your organization and assist in the cultivation of prospects. For those board members who shudder at the thought of asking people for money, you can assure them that their primary role is simply to help make introductions and cultivate friendships. If necessary, you or another advancement official can be prepared to make any asks.

Formalize your procedure for involving board members in this friend-making process by developing a form similar to the example at right. At a regularly scheduled board meeting, ask board members to complete and return it to you within a specified number of days. Then be prepared to begin following up with each board member immediately. (It's important to act while the assignment is still fresh in their minds.)

When you distribute the form, be sure to include your last honor roll of contributors so board members will be sure not to include names of those who are presently contributing to your organization. Better yet, also include a list of nondonors who would be likely prospect candidates.

---

### FRIEND-MAKING OBJECTIVES FOR BOARD MEMBERS
#### Confidential

*The purpose of this project is to involve all board members in making introductions and cultivating relationships with nondonors capable of making gifts of $10,000 or more. Your ability to help establish a positive relationship with friends and associates will help broaden our base of future major gift support as we plan for the future.*

*Our goal is to make individual introductory visits with each person you have identified within the next three months. Subsequent visits and objectives will be determined once initial calls have been completed.*

*Please identify three or more prospects (individuals, businesses or foundations) — who are presently non donors — capable of contributing $10,000 or more to our organization. We ask that you complete this form within the next week and return it to [Name].*

*Once your form is received, the appropriate development officer will contact you to begin coordinating available dates and times to set appointments with the persons you have identified.*

Your Name _____ Date _____

**1. Prospect** _____

Your Relationship to the Prospect: _____

Helpful Background Information (e.g., occupation, title, source of wealth):
_____

**2. Prospect** _____

Your Relationship to the Prospect: _____

Helpful Background Information: _____
_____

**3. Prospect** _____

Your Relationship to the Prospect: _____
Helpful Background Information: _____
_____

---

## Connect Board Members and Donors

Being formally saluted by your board is a great way to recognize major contributors.

If you're not already doing so, why not piggyback a meal or reception with all regularly scheduled board meetings? Invite recent major donors to the gathering to meet and be recognized by your board. Then prior to or following the gathering, guests can be dismissed and your board meeting can take place as scheduled.

Your guests will leave knowing they have just been thanked by your organization's leadership, and your board will take greater ownership.

## Tips for Gaining Your Board's Respect

In your efforts to raise funds, how are you familiarizing yourself with individuals and businesses that surround your nonprofit?

Get to know your neighbors whether residences or businesses. Having them on your side may one day result in their:

✓ Making a gift in-kind — services and/or products.

✓ Volunteering in some capacity: sharing their expertise or becoming involved on a committee or advisory board.

✓ Making an outright or planned gift.

✓ Being more supportive when the time comes to make changes to your campus or facilities — changes that may require city approval.

## Save Board Meeting Time With Consent Agenda

Board meeting agendas regularly include routine items, such as minutes from the last meeting and minor procedural changes, that don't need any discussion time and only need to be approved by the board.

One way to keep these types of items from taking up valuable board meeting time is to add them to a consent agenda section in your meeting agenda so your board can review and discuss them all at once.

Examples of consent agenda items include final approval of proposals or reports, routine appointments to committees, or information-only reports.

Ideally, consent agenda items are sent to board members a few weeks before the meeting so that they can review them and get any of their questions answered, as well as to facilitate quick approval of the consent agenda during the meeting.

The consent agenda is placed near the top of the meeting agenda. During the meeting, the title of each item on the consent agenda is read aloud. The chair asks if any items need to be removed from the consent agenda for discussion. Board members who would like additional discussion of a particular consent agenda item can request that it be removed from the consent agenda by title. Requests for removal should be done prior to approval of the consent agenda and can be discussed either right away or later in the meeting.

After items are removed or if there are no removal requests, the board chair can state, for example: "If there is no objection, these items will be adopted." If no one makes an objection, the chair can state, for example: "As there are no objections, these items are adopted."

The board will need to adopt a rule of order in its bylaws allowing it to use the consent agenda process. This rule of order might include the types of items that can be

> ### Sample Consent Agenda Section
>
> Action requested: Motion to approve items listed on Consent Agenda.
>
> A. Minutes from Dec. 1, 2009 board meeting
>
> B. Approval of changes to bylaws discussed in Dec. 15, 2009 board teleconference
>
> C. Approval of John Poe's appointment as at-large member of board

included in a consent agenda, how those items should be sent to the board chair (mail or e-mail) and how far in advance of the meeting. It might also require that consent agenda items receive unanimous approval.

Examples of consent agenda language can be found in these PDF documents:

Thomaston Public Schools (Thomaston, CT), page 5 of this document: www.thomastonschools.org/policy/9325adp.pdf

Metro Vancouver, Burnaby, British Columbia, page 2 of this document: www.metrovancouver.org/boards/bylaws/Amending%20Bylaws/RD_Bylaw_1059.pdf

Cambria Community Services District (Cambria, CA), page 3 of this document: www.cambriacsd.org/Library/PDFs/BOARD%20OF%20DIRECTORS/6.09%20Approved%20Bylaws.pdf

Trinity University (San Antonio, TX) — www.trinity.edu/departments/academic_affairs/hb/facgvstr/uccbylaw.htm#cons2

*Building Your Board: How to Attract Financially-Capable Board Members and Engage Them in Fund Development.* Edited by Scott C. Stevenson. © 2010 Stevenson, Inc. Published 2010 by Stevenson, Inc.

## WHEN IT COMES TO BOARD GIVING

*If it's your goal to surpass all past fundraising efforts, then it's critical that you, over time, recruit board members who have the capacity and proclivity to make major gifts, both outright and planned. This attribute should overshadow all other board recruitment objectives if you are serious about wanting to raise big bucks. And prospective board members should have a clear understanding of what's expected of them prior to being asked to join your board. The board sets the precedent for gifts that follow. Simple as that.*

## Set Annual Goal for Board Gifts

If your organization has little history of fundraising, be sure to set an annual goal for board gifts. Without it, you will find it challenging, if not impossible, to raise the bar in terms of giving in subsequent years.

Have your board's development committee come up with a realistic yet challenging goal for annual board support. Point out that the board's level of annual support sets a precedent for others who give. Many nonprofit boards will even approve a minimum gift level that board members are expected to give (or get) on an annual basis.

When you share a written report of total gifts to date (for the year) at board meetings, include a separate line item that reflects board gifts to date in relation to the board's giving goal.

## Accountability Form Improves Board Member Giving

A simple form is boosting board member accountability and giving for the Make-A-Wish Foundation of the Mid-South (Memphis, TN).

Liz Larkin, president/CEO, says the board commitment contract (shown at right) has helped to significantly increase board gifts. In 2004, before implementing the form, Larkin says, only three of 14 board members gave at the wish sponsorship level ($5,000 and up). Today, 13 of the 14 give at least $5,000 annually.

Larkin collected forms from other Make-A-Wish chapters and, with three members of the board development committee, created the document to address their organization's specific needs. Now, board members are required to sign the form at the start of each fiscal year. Board member prospects are informed of this annual responsibility prior to joining the board.

In signing the form, board members are committing to "The Give" ($5,000 per board member), "The Get" (direct support gifts such as individuals, corporations, foundations, etc. to help offset daily operating expenses) and event support (agreeing to attend, raise sponsors, pledges, auction items and/or sell tickets for at least one of the organization's major events).

Larkin tracks members' progress with a board report card shared at board meetings that details how close they are to meeting their annual commitments to give funds and get support, as well as meeting attendance, fundraising help, board member recruitment, etc.

"If a board member is not meeting the expectations of giving their time, talents and treasures, then the board chair has a conversation with them," she says. "Typically, the board member will either resign or step up. The board members like the accountability."

*Source: Liz Larkin, President/CEO, Make-A-Wish Foundation of the Mid-South, Memphis, TN. Phone (901) 680-9474. E-mail: llarkin@midsouth.wish.org*

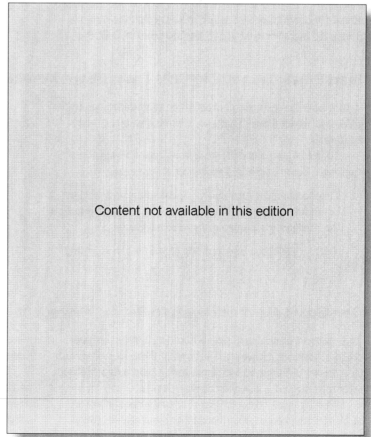

Content not available in this edition

## Engage Your Board in Selecting Their Funding Project

Want to raise the level of annual giving among your board members? Involve them in a process that allows them to select their own funding project.

Begin with your staff by identifying a list of potential projects the board might find appealing. Select only those projects whose price tag is high enough to stretch board giving. If, for example, you have 15 board members and it's your hope to raise the yearly average board gift to $1,500, select projects that can't get realized without a cumulative commitment of $22,500 or more.

In addition, make it clear that the project they select will not be made possible unless the goal is fully reached by a particular date.

After developing a handful of funding projects, present them to your board's development committee to review and discuss. If this committee understands and owns what you are attempting to accomplish, they will be better equipped to sell the remaining board members when it comes time to selecting and approving a funding project.

## Increase Annual Gifts From Your Board Members

 *"What are you doing to get your board members to make annual gifts at higher levels?"*

"Consider using what is known as a 'wrap-around' method. If your organization is in a capital campaign, a donor's annual fund gift is wrapped around their capital fund gift. That's assuming that your organization is steadfast in retaining its annual fund during a capital campaign.

"Here's how it works: Say a board member of a nonprofit makes a $50,000 contribution to your capital campaign over five years, this concept would ask the donor to devote $40,000 to the capital campaign and $10,000 to the annual fund over that time frame. The $10,000 gift to the annual fund would be structured in a way that the donor's gift would increase each year. The first year, $1,000; the

second year, $1,500; the third year, $2,000; the fourth year, $2,500; and the fifth year, $3,000.

"For those organizations not in a capital campaign, the concept works somewhat the same. Asking board members who are in a three- or five-year term to make a commitment the first year donating $1,000 and each year thereafter, increasing the gift in $500 increments.

"We have used this concept in our previous three capital campaigns and it has worked very effectively. For example, the current capital campaign goal is $30 million, we currently have 100 percent participation from our board who contributed $9 million of that goal."

— *Frank Pasquini, Vice President, Institutional Advancement, King's College, Wilkes-Barre, PA*

## Start Small to Land Big Gifts From Board Members

If your board members fall short when it comes to generous gifts, you're not alone. That's an ailment that faces many nonprofits.

To get larger gifts from your board, take a long-term approach. Some upgrading strategies may include:

1. Turn to the most financially capable members of your board and convince them how a major gift will help raise the bar among remaining board members.

2. Guide your board nominations committee in selecting only those individuals who have the financial capacity to give at higher levels. Make that a priority for nomination.

3. Convince someone — an individual, foundation or current board member — to establish a board challenge whereby all board gifts over a certain dollar amount will be matched.

4. Make any decision to launch a capital campaign hinge on the board's agreement to underwrite at least one quarter of the campaign goal.

## One Board Member Needs to Set the Precedent

You can have a who's who of individuals serving on your board of trustees. However, until one of them steps forward with an unprecedented, sacrificial gift, others may very well refrain from giving at highly capable levels.

Work at convincing that most capable board member of his/her role before other board members step up to the plate with less-than-desirable pledges. Help that single board member realize the potential he/she possesses.

Paint a picture of what could be versus what's probable without that level of leadership. Your shared vision should depict specific examples of how your organization will achieve greatness with a great gift.

## Characteristics of a Campaign-ready Board

For your board to be ready for a capital campaign, its members must recognize and understand the critical role they will play in its success. So how will you know when they have arrived? What characteristics will manifest themselves among the campaign-ready board?

A board committed to campaign success will have members who:

- Own your strategic plan because they helped design it.
- Are prepared to make their own sacrificial leadership gifts first.
- Have major gift solicitation experience.

- Willingly attend campaign meetings and make solicitation calls.
- Recognize successful campaigns are elitist, not populist.
- Make realistic commitments of time and knowledge.
- Grasp the quiet phase strategy of a major campaign.
- Maintain momentum and enthusiasm throughout the campaign.
- Know the bulk of support comes from individuals, not corporations or foundations.
- Are committed to the campaign and recruit others to help

## Unlock Your Board's Campaign Potential

Knowing board gifts can account for a third or more of a capital campaign goal, and recognizing that board support establishes the precedent for gifts to follow, what steps can and should you take to prepare board members for unprecedented campaign gifts?

How can you raise your board's sights as you gear up for a campaign?

Assuming you already have a board in place that includes financially capable trustees, here are some top recommendations from *The Major Gifts Report's* panel of experts for encouraging those board members to give at their full potential:

1. Be sure board members are part of an ongoing strategic planning process. If they are to commit to an ambitious and successful campaign, they need to own the entire process that leads up to that event. Include them — both collectively and individually — in designing a long-term plan for your organization. Help them understand the need for additional resources and what the realization of those resources can accomplish.

2. Make board members aware of what other successful nonprofits have achieved. To help raise the sights of your board, share examples of what other charities have accomplished with campaigns. The more examples they see, the more they will understand that they, too, can do the same.

3. Your pre-campaign vision should include lofty goals. If you think small, your board members will do the same. Instead, everyone needs to reach for goals that will stretch them beyond what they believed capable

of themselves. Board members need to believe that the identified goals are critical and must be achieved to adequately fulfill the organization's mission. You can always pare back goals if necessary, but it's nearly impossible to do the opposite once a strategic plan has been established.

4. Cultivate the attention of key board members prior to conducting a feasibility study. Obviously the results of a feasibility study — based on individual and group interviews that include board members — determine the final campaign goal. That's why it's important in advance of the study to cultivate individual interest in the campaign with those board members whose financial ability can set a precedent for other board members to follow. Meet one-on-one to measure their interest in the campaign as well as in specific giving opportunities. Develop a sense of those persons' potential interests before the feasibility study takes place. Convince them that the magnitude of an eventual campaign will be determined, in part, by the example they set for others.

5. Approach board members sequentially based on both gift capability and inclination to give. Once the feasibility study has been completed and a goal recommended to the full board, approach first those few board members whose sacrificial pledges will send a clear signal to others that this campaign is more significant than any previous effort in the organization's history.

Many facets of the pre-campaign phase are important, but if your board members cannot become passionate about the effort and their individual responsibilities in making it a success, it might be best to rethink your plans.

## Can Your Board Fund a Third of Your Campaign Goal?

**Case Study: You want to launch a major campaign in 2013, but there's a problem. You have a board made up mostly of individuals who have neither the capacity nor the inclination to make major gifts. What to do?**

First of all, you need to know that it's not uncommon for a successful campaign to realize anywhere from one-third to one-half of its goal from both current and former board members. So you have three years to transform your board into a precedent-setting group of generous donors. Can it be done? With focus and determination, yes.

Here's a very basic outline of what you'll need to do:

1. First, identify any current and former board members who have the capability to make a significant gift. If you come up with no one, evaluate your charity's pool of nonboard donors to identify such a person or persons.

2. Begin to cultivate that individual or handful of individuals about the need for methodically and selectively recruiting financially capable board members. If they are not already on your board, do what's necessary to get them elected.

3. Help those few insiders realize their primary goal is to identify, cultivate and recruit others of means who will join your board and become actively engaged in its work.

4. At the same time this handful of members is working to stack the deck, ask them to begin pressuring existing board members by proposing minimum annual contributions. This forces current board members to either rise to the occasion or resign.

Although the process of transforming a board is much more complex than the steps outlined here, seeing it described in this simplistic manner can help you to begin to tackle the board transformation challenge head on.

---

### Useful Board Exercise

Explain to your board that you want to garner relationship-building ideas as you meet with would-be donors. To accomplish that, ask them to answer the following question: What might cause you to make a significant gift?

In addition to getting ideas, their responses may provide you with clues to their proclivity to give.

---

### Teach Your Board About Sacrificial Giving

While not all board members can contribute at the same level, each is capable of making a sacrificial gift — a gift amounting to more than the board member realized he/she was capable of giving.

Identify various ways to teach board members about sacrificial gifts — a guest editorial in your newsletter or magazine, or a testimonial at your next board meeting from one who has made a sacrificial gift.

When you can identify someone who has made a stretch gift, recognize him/her in the presence of other board members.

---

### Weigh Options, Scope of Board Challenge Gifts

Approaching a board member for a challenge gift can sometimes serve to "stretch" the member's own giving. But before making an approach, weigh the options to be sure you're getting the most bang for your challenge buck.

For example, should you approach just one board member for a challenge gift? Who would most be motivated by a challenge gift? Or, should you approach two, three or four members to establish a combined challenge gift?

---

### Is Your Board Chair Active?

What are you doing — by design — to involve your board chairperson in the cultivation, solicitation and/or stewardship of major gifts? Put your plans for that position in writing, and follow them.

## Help Top Board Members Realize Their Potential

Knowing that as much as 60 percent of a capital campaign goal can be realized through current and former board members' gifts, what are you doing to help individual board members realize their potential as transformational donors — those whose gifts could transform your organization?

Cultivate board members toward the realization of transformational gifts by:

- Sharing examples of others who have made such gifts to various charities. Demonstrate the before and after of such gifts.

- Developing a strategic plan — with their involvement — that creates a lofty vision of what could be with the proper level of support.

## Convince Board Members To Make Stretch Gifts

Requiring 100 percent board giving may get your board members to contribute, but how much? Sometimes requiring all board members to give isn't enough to encourage them to make stretch gifts.

Get your board to go along with a dollar goal. Let members know that reaching the goal will help the organization land foundation gifts. Begin personal solicitation of board members with that in mind.

## A Word of Caution About Board-funded Projects

Knowing your board members' gifts should raise the bar for all other gifts that follow, it's generally unwise to invite your board to collectively fund a particular project.

Group-funded projects sometimes allow board members to give less than they would as individuals. They also tend to discourage stretch giving.

If you do invite your board to underwrite a particular project:

- Make the group funding project a giving opportunity that is in addition to what board members are asked to contribute as individuals.

- Consider asking the board chair to impose a minimum gift amount so a few board members don't end up carrying the load for everyone else.

## Convince Board Members to Make Planned Gifts

It's worth your investment of time to convince board members to make planned gifts to your organization.

Why, you ask? Several reasons:

1. If board members aren't sold on the value of planned gifts to your organization, how can they expect others to make such gifts?

2. Likewise, board members who have made planned gift provisions will be much better equipped to sell others on the idea.

3. Board members — more than any other constituency — should realize the tremendous good that can be accomplished through the realization of major planned gifts over time.

The more your board members own your planned gifts program, the more likely they are to set an example for others to follow.

Here are some strategies you can use to convince your

board members to make planned gifts to your organization:

- Enlist assistance of existing planned gift donors to help sell your board.

- Use regular meetings to educate board members on various aspects of planned gifts — types of gifts, ways they can be directed, naming opportunities and so forth.

- If you have a planned gifts society, invite board members to help host its events.

- Use board meetings to recognize those having made planned gifts.

- Ask individual board members to help in identifying planned gift prospects.

- List the names of your board on all planned gifts materials — brochures, letterhead, newsletters, etc.

- Get your board to own and endorse your planned gifts policies and procedures.

## Get Board Buy-in

If you want your board to buy into a challenge gift, get your board to approve it before it becomes official! Board members' odds of contributing to the challenge will increase if they give it the go ahead first.

## Four Steps to a Powerful Board

Your board's collective reputation can help attract major gifts. While capacity to give should be a top priority when recruiting candidates, public perception is also key. CEOs, successful entrepreneurs or other well-known and respected leaders add immediate clout.

To transform a typical board into a powerful one:

1. **Draft a timetable and internal action plan.** Recognize that board transformation takes time — up to five years. Map out a plan to identify and engage board candidates who fit your expectations with regard to financial capability, connections and reputation.

2. **Start by forging relationships with two or three powerful individuals.** Go to existing donors to uncover connections to persons of power and wealth. Ask them to introduce you and cultivate relationships. Look for persons with corporate or personal interests that match your mission.

3. **Tell it like it is.** Explain to these individuals that you want to build your board's stature and that doing so will require attracting one or two or three individuals such as themselves willing to help enlist others of similar prominence.

4. **Use first board recruits to approach and enlist others.** Appoint them to your board nominations committee. Emphasize that their primary role is to identify and positively influence others to join your board. In addition to financial support, they are to be catalysts in reaching out to others.

## Board Chairman's Strong Belief Challenges Others to Give

In the midst of a comprehensive campaign for Lycoming College (Williamsport, PA), Chairman of the Board Arthur Haberberger and his wife Joanne proposed a new program to target donors who are considering their first outright major gift.

At Lycoming College the threshold for an endowed scholarship is $25,000. The Chairman's Challenge is an opportunity for prospective donors to establish a scholarship at the $20,000 level.

"The challenge is a generous commitment by the Haberbergers to help donors interested in starting a new scholarship reach the $25,000 minimum commitment," says Jennifer Wilson, director of development. "For every gift of $20,000, they will invest $5,000 toward a new endowed scholarship."

The couple has committed to seeing 50 new scholarships created, which, if realized, would mean $1.25 million in endowed scholarships for Lycoming. Since announcing the program in spring 2007, Wilson says they have averaged one new scholarship a month as a direct result of the challenge.

The development office works with the donor to develop the criteria (e.g., preference to students in certain academic fields or by geographic area). The name of the scholarship is also the donor's choice and can be named after a family member, in memory of a loved one, or themselves.

With the college in its active campaign solicitation, development office staff worked to identify potential scholarship donors through prospect meetings and talks with staff to identify prospects based on past giving and conversations with donors. "This challenge provided us a great opportunity to work with donors on taking the next step to a major gift," says Wilson.

They also marketed the program in the college magazine, campaign newsletter and in a brochure (shown below) developed specifically for the Chairman's Challenge as a leave-behind piece after solicitations.

Donors have the option to make their gift outright or fulfill their pledge commitment within three to five years.

*Source: Jennifer Wilson, Director of Development, Lycoming College, Williamsport, PA. Phone (570) 321-4395. E-mail: wilson@lycoming.edu*

Content not available in this edition

*Building Your Board: How to Attract Financially-Capable Board Members and Engage Them in Fund Development.* Edited by Scott C. Stevenson.
© 2010 Stevenson, Inc. Published 2010 by Stevenson, Inc.

## CONTINUE TO NURTURE, INFORM YOUR BOARD

*You can't simply terminate one group of board members and bring in a fresh slate of individuals. It's not that simple. The process of identifying, recruiting and educating board members is ongoing. It requires using different approaches to engage and motivate both existing and new board members. Your board should possess ownership not only of your organization and its work, but also of your fund development efforts. While approving development related policies is important, it's not enough.*

## Six Techniques to Nurture Board Ownership of Your Charity, Its Programs

Board members are much more likely to give of their time, talents and treasures if they assume more ownership in your organization, its programs and services.

Here are six tangible ways to boost board members' knowledge of and involvement in your nonprofit:

1. **Initiate a yearly adoption program** for board members to adopt a particular department and get to know your nonprofit better through staff and those who benefit from its programs and services.

2. **Incorporate continuing education** into regular board meetings. Invite employee groups to make a brief presentation on an aspect of your organization. Presenters may even wish to share a display that gives board members a chance to browse and learn more about a particular program, accomplishment or need.

3. **Meet individually with board members** to learn more about their interests so you can better match them with appealing projects.

4. **Invite board members to sit in on special meetings** that may interest them. If, for instance, you've scheduled an advancement staff meeting to discuss a planned event or fundraising strategies, invite one or two board members to sit in and listen — even offer suggestions.

5. **Selectively feed written materials** to all or key board members, choosing information to increase their understanding of issues directly impacting your nonprofit as well as broader issues (e.g., legislation, demographics).

6. **Provide focused tours** that expose board members to a specific area of your nonprofit's work.

## Help Your CEO Groom Board Members

When it comes to fund development, one of the CEO's primary responsibilities is to cultivate and, in some instances, solicit board members. And it is the responsibility of the development office to support him/her toward that end. To do that effectively:

1. Meet with your CEO on at least a monthly basis to review activities of each board member during the past 30 days, and discuss specific strategies for the next 60 days. Agree to the primary objective of each planned visit.

2. Be mindful of keeping your CEO apprised of individual board members' happenings: birthdays, anniversaries, promotions and more.

3. Be willing to arrange board appointments and coordinate board events on his/her behalf.

4. Provide the CEO with a written brief of key information about board members on whom he/she will be calling.

5. Offer to accompany your boss on particular board visits where it might be helpful to have a second individual present.

6. Equally as important as cultivation and solicitation, see that your CEO is properly stewarding those board members who have made generous gifts. That means personal attention geared to each donor's particular interests and circumstances.

## Meet One-on-one With Board Members

From a development standpoint, regularly meeting one-on-one with your board members makes sense.

In the face-to-face sessions, you can:

✓ Review fiscal year giving to date.
✓ Talk key issues/challenges at hand.
✓ Brainstorm about whom to approach for a challenge gift.
✓ Address funding interests of individual board members.

✓ Identify their associates/friends who might merit a personal visit.
✓ Come up with new ways to address your nonprofit's strategic plans from a fundraising standpoint.
✓ Toss around ways in which the board can positively participate in and impact development events/programs, especially major and planned gifts.

## Match Board Members' Strengths With Projects to Create Energy

It's unproductive to have a universal set of fund development expectations for board members. Rather than dictate how they can help fundraising efforts, why not energize them by matching their individual strengths, connections and interests with projects that can make a positive difference?

Work with each board member to identify projects each can take on as personal goals. Some may be short-term tasks while others are more long-term in nature.

Examples may include but not be limited to:

✓ Identifying and cultivating relationships with a handful of individuals or business decision makers capable of making major gifts.

✓ Hosting events aimed at attracting new prospects to your cause.

✓ Writing editorials or testimonials that make the case for supporting your cause.

✓ Helping to steward existing donors.

✓ Making inroads with particular foundations through existing peer relationships.

## Focus Cultivation Efforts on Few Who Will Raise the Bar

Want to convince more board members to give at higher levels? Focus your cultivation efforts on those few board members who possess the capacity and proclivity to give more generously.

If you build a group of board members committed to major gifts, their example will motivate remaining board members to do more.

Whether your attention is geared to a particular board member or a few, here's how to get them to step up to the plate:

1. Get that board member to establish a sizeable challenge gift to match new and increased gifts from other board members.

2. After he/she makes a large gift, convince that board member to be your spokesperson who encourages fellow board members to give at higher levels or get off the board.

3. Engage board members in identifying a funding project that the full board can buy into and realize through their collective gifts.

4. Convince your targeted board members to propose a board-only gift club that is limited to those board members who give at a certain level. Allow inclusion of emeritus board members as well.

## Nurture Board Productivity

A common complaint among nonprofit workers is that their board isn't fully engaged in fundraising efforts. Likewise, board members complain about not being fully utilized.

So how do you bridge that gap and get your board on board?

Make specific requests of board members rather than just asking them to help in general terms, advises Dana Kindrick, executive administrative assistant, Navarro College Foundation (Corsicana, TX).

Linking board members to specific projects allows them to make their own best contribution. The following tips can help:

❑ **Know your board.** Every member should have a defined purpose prior to being asked to sit on a board. An attorney may help rewrite bylaws. A financial planner may help with planned gifts. Without defined roles, it's hard for board members to be effective.

❑ **Really know your board.** Fully vet your prospective board members. Don't be afraid to ask specifics about how many hours per month they can donate, what relationships they have that may be valuable to your cause and what roles they see themselves taking. This will not scare off true prospects, and if it does, you're better off with that happening now than halfway through your capital campaign.

❑ **Make sure they know you.** Be clear about expectations before a prospective member accepts your offer. Have a set job description, guidelines for minimum board gifts and expected time commitment to help them make an informed decision.

❑ **Do an annual needs assessment for your board.** When you formally evaluate your board, you might be surprised to find you have four attorneys, but no financial planners. You might have a board full of people donating their own money, but are uncomfortable asking others to donate. An honest evaluation will help you correct those situations for a more balanced and productive board.

*Source: Dana Kindrick, Executive Administrative Assistant, Navarro College Foundation, Corsicana, TX.*
*Phone (903) 875-7591. E-mail: dana.kindrick@navarrocollege.edu*

## Keep Board Informed With a Dedicated Intranet

Looking to increase the efficiency and effectiveness of board members, staff and volunteers? Consider streamlining information and resource sharing with a dedicated organizational intranet.

"It's a private online space where stakeholders can find everything from time cards to information on current and prospective grants," explains Lee Ann Kim, executive director of the San Diego Asian Film Foundation (SDAFF), which has utilized such a system for almost a decade.

The resources board members can find on the SDAFF intranet include lists of staff contact information, detailed biographies of other board members, and meeting schedules and calendars. Financial information such as recent audits and current 501(c)(3) statements is also available. But more importantly, the foundation also puts sponsorship records at the disposal of board members.

"Savvy fundraisers can click on any of the 500 or so sponsors that have supported us over the last 12 years and see their history of giving, any recent interactions with us, and a current name and contact number," says Kim. "They never have to wonder if this or that company is on board with a project."

From a technical standpoint, the user interface is remarkably straightforward, with new board members authorized to choose their own username and password. And because the system is designed around tiered levels of access, the accounts of former board members need not be deleted — they are simply transferred to a more limited level of access.

The system, custom built for the foundation in 2002, was revolutionary for its time. But while it still offers many advantages, Kim says applications like Googledocs have come to approximate many of its functions.

"Not every nonprofit can design their own system from the ground up, but these programs are incredibly easy to use and absolutely free. They can be a real lifesaver," she says. "I would definitely recommend them to anyone."

*Source: Lee Ann Kim, Executive Director, San Diego Asian Film Foundation, San Diego, CA. Phone (858) 565-1264. E-mail: Leeann@sdaff.org. Website: http://www.sdaff.org*

## Educate Board Members About Top Contributors

At least quarterly, inform your board members of the top 10 to 20 major contributors to your organization, says Jean Block, president of Jean Block Consulting, Inc., (Albuquerque, NM). Include a brief bio and current photo, if available.

Doing so can only improve your donor relations, Block says, while potentially eliminating embarrassing faux pas.

"If your board members don't know your top contributors and are one day sitting next to one of them," she says, "the donor will be sitting there wondering when the board member is going to say thank-you."

*Source: Jean Block, President, Jean Block Consulting, Inc., Albuquerque, NM. Phone (505) 899-1520. E-mail: jean@jblockinc.com*

## Spoon-feed Your Board

As you work to build a board that assumes an active role in fund development, take every opportunity to educate, engage and motivate board members, collectively and individually. Incorporate these motivating measures into your contacts with them:

- Ask a seasoned volunteer solicitor — even if he/she represents another nonprofit — to speak to your board.

- Give regular and public recognition to board members who assist (in any way) in fund development.

- Invite board members to make thank-you calls on recent donors as a way to become more comfortable interacting with donors.

- Cite examples of how other volunteers' willingness to identify and/or cultivate prospects resulted in new gifts for your organization.

- Offer multiple opportunities for board members to invite guests to tour and get involved with your organization.

- Seek board input on challenges facing your fundraising efforts.

## Board Cultivation Idea

At least once a year, provide each board member with an individual tour of your facilities, allowing him/her to observe your nonprofit in action. Occasionally stop and visit with an employee and pose a question about the employee's work.

    This process allows board members to see your organization in action and witness its important work while helping to uncover individual funding interests of these key players.

## Keep Your Board Apprised Of Direct Mail Appeals

It's good to keep your board members aware of appeals that are being sent out. Here are a few ways to do that without inundating them with copies of all of your annual fund mailings:

- Share the basic messages of your mailings along with a copy of brochures or other printed materials that will accompany the letters, individually, if asked.

- Include a summary of your mailing plan and the messages for the year in board members' meeting packets.

## Teach Board Members to Have Fun Soliciting Gifts

Board members will be more eager to assist in soliciting major gifts if they find the experience enjoyable. That's why it makes sense to incorporate fun into your board's solicitation efforts.

    The following techniques will help to make board members' asking assignments more pleasant and energizing:

- Invite board members to make calls in teams of two. That makes the task more palatable and strengthens board camaraderie.

- Incorporate some competition among individual board members and board teams (e.g., largest gift solicited, most new pledges during a quarter, most difficult prospect

award). Provide regular updates on who's in the lead.

- Make time to celebrate solicitation victories along the way. Recognize individual and team successes.

- Allow time at meetings for board members to share anecdotes of completed calls.

- Mix in thank-you calls with solicitation calls. Thanking donors is rewarding.

- During a training session, conduct a demonstration of the right way and wrong way to solicit a major gift. Have fun with this, incorporating humor into the example of what not to do.

## What Ignites Your Board?

Your board members should set the bar for all others when it comes to giving. Help them do so by identifying opportunities that will cause them to make major gifts.

    Use these techniques to uncover funding opportunities that ignite them:

1. Periodically take each board member on a facilities tour to see programs and services in action. Observe what captures the person's attention.

2. Meet one-on-one to learn more about what makes the

person tick. What has most impacted the person's life?

3. Observe how they act at board meetings. What questions are they asking? What agenda topics are most attracting their attention?

4. Set up situations that allow individual board members to interact with those you serve and pick up on clues that may point to funding interests.

5. Invite board members to actively participate in strategic planning meetings.

*Building Your Board: How to Attract Financially-Capable Board Members and Engage Them in Fund Development.* Edited by Scott C. Stevenson. © 2010 Stevenson, Inc. Published 2010 by Stevenson, Inc.

*Following are several tried-and-tested ideas from our editors and other nonprofit organizations that you may want to consider as you work to build and nurture a financially capable, can-do board of your own. Continue to set high expectations for your board. Meet regularly with them, both collectively and individually. Ask for their involvement. Engage them in fund development.*

## Anticipated-trips Form Plugs Board Members Into Cultivation Process

Do you have a board member making a business trip to the East or West Coast? What about the retired board member who vacations in Florida each winter?

Why not take advantage of your board members' — and other close friends of your organization — travels by involving them in the cultivation process of major gift prospects who live far away?

Utilization of an anticipated-trips form will help you pinpoint opportunities to involve board members and others in identifying, cultivating, researching and even soliciting gifts on your behalf.

Here are a few activities with which traveling board members could assist you:

- Hosting a reception
- Conducting prospect research on individuals, businesses or foundations in that region
- Making introductory calls
- Delivering a message of thanks for past support
- Hand delivering a proposal
- Seeking donated items for events

Rather than sending the forms, distribute them at board meetings to explain how helpful their involvement can be with these out-of-town prospects. Share the forms selectively with others who travel in affluent circles.

Once the form is completed and turned in, staff can identify appropriate fund development activities and discuss them before departure.

Sharing this form with board members and others will have multiple benefits:

- Completed forms help to keep your office posted on the schedules of board members and others.
- By involving these persons in the fund development process, you are also engaging them — helping them more fully own the role of major gifts at your institution.
- Their involvement will help accomplish cultivation, research and solicitation that otherwise might not have been accomplished.

These traveling ambassadors can help do their part to enhance the image and work of your organization throughout the nation.

*Sample anticipated-trips form that board members and others can complete to assist in the cultivation on distant prospects.*

---

RANDOM UNIVERSITY
Anticipated-trips Form

*Designed for board members and other Random University "insiders" who wish to serve as ambassadors during their business and leisure travels.*

*When a trip is planned, simply complete this form and turn it into the Institutional Advancement Office. A development officer will then contact you to go over possible ways in which you could assist in making contacts with individuals.*

Name _____

Trip Destination _____
❑ Business    ❑ Pleasure

Dates of Trip
Arrival Date _____ Departure Date _____

Where You Can Be Reached
Address _____
_____

Phone ( ___ ) _____ Fax ( ___ ) _____

Examples of Ambassador activities with which you might assist:

❑ Introductory visits
    ❑ With individuals
    ❑ With business representatives
    ❑ With foundations

❑ Friendship-building activities    ❑ Distributing literature about Random University

❑ Hosting a reception    ❑ Identifying potential contributors

❑ Telephoning friends/donors of the university    ❑ Soliciting a gift

❑ Delivering a proposal    ❑ Securing donated items for our annual gala

❑ Other (Please describe) _____
_____
_____
_____

---

## Survey Allows for Anonymous Board Feedback

Here's one way to solicit anonymous feedback from board members about what they feel is working — and what isn't — for your organization, your board, your reputation in the community and other elements of your nonprofit:

Prior to your next board meeting, send surveys to board members. Emphasize that all responses are to be anonymous and should be typed on white paper — with no names — guaranteeing their anonymity. Ask them to bring the answer sheet to the next scheduled meeting and place them in a ballot type box that you place outside of the meeting room. Don't open the box until you return to your office.

This method ensures that board members won't be identifiable through their handwriting; no one can get a peek at their responses; and because they all look alike, you won't be able to tell, even if you are there when they put the paper into the box, whose survey response is whose once the box is opened.

## Get Board Members Involved in Raising Major Gifts

Plot ways to engage key players in your major fundraising efforts to maximize success.

As a way to get board members involved in its campaign, for example, staff with The Clinic (Phoenixville, PA), a medical center for the uninsured, asks board members to handwrite short notes to donors they know.

The notes, written on 2-by-4-inch notepads printed with The Clinic's logo, are included in direct-mail solicitation letters sent to major donors. All board members participate, each writing about a dozen notes.

"Board members may write something positive like, 'We hope you can help us out,' or 'I look forward to seeing you at the next event,'" says Debbie Shupp, development director. "These notes add a personal touch to our mailings."

Board members also write notes to include in event invitations for the major donors they know, says Shupp, who notes: "For our last golf outing, we probably wouldn't have had 80 percent of our sponsors if we did not have board involvement in inviting the sponsors."

*Source: Debbie Shupp, Development Director, The Clinic, Phoenixville, PA. Phone (610) 935-1134 ext. 24. E-mail: dshupp@theclinicpa.org*

## Get One Board Member Who Will Champion Your Cause

If your nonprofit has little history of securing major gifts, one of the most important steps you can take is to enlist a financially capable board member who knows and is respected by others of means. If that person does nothing more than to help identify and attract other board members, he/she will have made a significant contribution to your cause.

Here's one approach for enlisting such an individual:

1. First, review your inner circle of most generous contributors. Who among them already has an affinity to the work of your charity? Your champion will hopefully reside within this group. If not, you may need to look for another who has a history of philanthropy to other causes within your community and begin to cultivate his/her interest. This latter option may have equal potential to the first but will require more time nurturing his/her interest and involvement.

2. Begin meeting individually with your top three or four choices. Explain that your goal is to bring someone of his/her stature on board with the sole intent of identifying, cultivating and enlisting others of means to join your board or to eventually make a major gift.

3. As you meet with each potential champion, be up front and specific about your expectations: "I would like you to give at least one year of your time — meeting on a monthly basis — to identify and cultivate 10 individuals who have the capability of making $10,000-and-above gifts to our charity."

4. Once an individual has agreed to work with you, meet regularly to review names and discuss possible approaches for each prospect the two of you identify. Offer to accompany your champion on calls, but be clear that he/she will be key at making introductions and being involved in the friend-building process.

By following this procedure with one willing individual throughout the course of a year, you will be building a foundation that will result in attracting capable individuals who will one day invest generously in your cause.

## Form a Gift Acceptance Committee

What formal structure do you have in place to accept major gifts in all their forms?

Safe Horizon (New York, NY) has a five-person gift acceptance committee (GAC) that reviews and decides whether to accept non-routine gifts.

The organization's gift acceptance policy defines non-routine gifts as any gift other than cash, cash pledges or publicly traded securities. "Even gifts of cash, cash pledges and publicly traded securities are reviewed if they come from campaign funds of politicians or if they are contributions intended to create permanently restricted accounts," says Christopher Moore, director of marketing and communication.

Safe Horizon's GAC is comprised of the organization's chief executive officer, general counsel, senior vice president for development, chief financial and administrative officer and chief development officer.

The committee will call on other individuals for advice on an as-needed basis depending on the nature of the proposed gift, says Moore. "These other individuals may be internal, such as someone from our Domestic Violence Shelters program, or external, such as an appraiser or other expert."

The CEO serves as chair of the GAC, but the meetings are called and conducted by the development department, he says, namely the chief development officer or senior vice president for development, on a case-by-case basis.

"Unusual or inappropriate gifts aren't offered frequently," notes Moore, "so regularly scheduled meetings have not been necessary."

*Source: Christopher Moore, Director of Marketing and Communication, Safe Horizon, New York, NY. Phone (212) 577-7700. E-mail: Christopher.moore@safehorizon.org*

## Key Into Board Members' Interests, Hobbies

Do you really know what your board members like doing for fun? How they enjoy spending their free time? What particular interests or hobbies they pursue?

Use those personal interests as a starting point for what may result in a major gift. To get started:

- **Identify their personal interests.** When meeting one-on-one, explore board members' interests or hobbies. Find out what energizes them. Do they have a pilot's license and like to fly? Are they into stamp collecting? Ballroom dancing? Are they fans of a particular college or professional sports team?

- **Look for ways to match their interests with your nonprofit's work.** Perhaps they would like to exhibit a collection in your lobby or speak to a volunteer or other group about their hobby. Or maybe their mutual support of your cause and a beloved sports team could lead to their sponsoring a visit by a popular coach or other sports celebrity for your special event.

By tuning into board members' personal interests, you may be amazed at how you can capture their attention and turn it into a relationship-strengthening opportunity that will blossom into a major gift.

## Ask Board Members to Secure $1,000-plus Donors

To broaden your base of future major donors, turn to your board. Ask each board member to identify, cultivate and solicit three annual gifts of $1,000 or more this fiscal year.

Although you or other staff may need to assist each board member in various ways — identification, strategizing, accompanying them on calls — this expectation gets board members to assume greater ownership in fund development. They will, by their very

**Do the Math:** 20 board members each securing three gifts of $1,000 or more throughout your fiscal year would result in 60 new $1,000 contributors. That's 60 new donors capable of one day making a major gift.

involvement, be more enthusiastic about wanting to achieve fundraising success, and will likely become more committed donors themselves.

## Hold a Thank-a-thon to Recognize Donors, Recharge Board Members

Does the thought of coordinating an organized effort to thank your many donors seem overwhelming and time consuming? Consider a Thank-a-Thon, a technique that works well for Jewish Family Service of Greater Dallas (Dallas, TX).

Every two or three months, Development Director Amy Walton organizes the thank-a-thon, in which board members call donors of all gift sizes with a personal message of thanks, answer questions they have and invite them to come for a personal tour. Over two hours, five or six board members are able to make more than 200 calls, Walton says.

In an effort to stay connected with lapsed contributors, in fall 2008 Walton had board members call donors who gave in 2006 or 2007 but had not yet given in 2008. The calls were strictly to say thanks, she says, but if the donor explicitly asks how to make a contribution, board members are able to provide options to do so.

Board member volunteers receive scripts and an information card (prepared using Microsoft Word's catalogue function under Mail Merge; see example, right) for each donor referencing family names and recent gift history and has a space to make notes about the conversation to be entered into the organization's donor software.

"Amongst the sea of direct mail, holiday cards, bills and more, we want our donors to know that they are valued by Jewish Family Service," says Walton. "And even when they have to cut back or cut out giving (as many may have to do in these economic times), we still consider them to be a part of our family. Personal contact makes the donor feel special, and we find this kind of stewardship stands apart from the most eloquently written thank-you letter."

Board members who participate in the thank-a-thon are encouraged to attend annual fundraising training, but Walton says she always emphasizes that personal passion is all that is needed to be effective. "If they communicate why they contribute/volunteer/advocate for Jewish Family Service, it will resonate with those they interact with, whether it is a friend they see in the grocery store or a stranger they call during our thank-a-thon."

Board member Linda Garner, who has participated in three thank-a-thons, says the efforts are rewarding and reinforce her commitment to the organization. "Every single person thanks you for calling," she says. "Many of the donors I called said how nice it was to be thanked without being asked for anything in return."

Walton says not a thank-a-thon goes by without board members saying how rejuvenated they feel from the experience.

Thank-a-thons are held either before a board meeting or scheduled for a specific night. Walton says the group effort creates a more positive experience because they can feed off the positive energy of working together.

At calling sessions, volunteers meet for snacks and a brief visit, then staff do a quick orientation about the category of donors they'll be calling and how the thank-a-thon fits into the overall development cycle. Thank-a-Thon room signs are hung on doors of offices that board members can use to make calls by personal cell phone or office phone line.

*Source: Amy Walton, Development Director; Robin Sachs, Board President; and Linda Garner, Board Member, Jewish Family Service, Dallas, TX. Phone (972) 437-9950, ext. 209.*

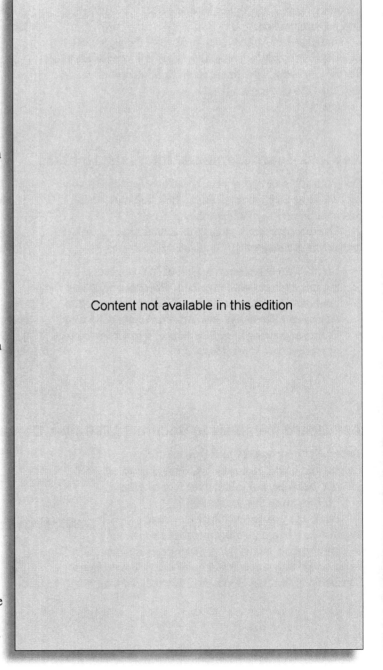

Content not available in this edition

## Help Volunteer Board Understand Solicitation Role

Major gifts success starts and ends with inside support. But what if your current volunteer-based board is not as clearly focused on raising major gifts as you would prefer?

Here, three fundraising experts share their insight on how to reshape your volunteer-based board into one more focused on fundraising:

*Sondra Dellaripa, Vice President of Development, Eastern Connecticut Health Network (Hartford, CT):*

Rather than looking for ways to change your board, realize that your board members must want to change themselves. "Developing the case for change must start with board members' understanding and belief that to change is far more important to the existence of their organization than to stay the same," says Dellaripa.

She suggests finding a board champion to help you deliver this message to other board members. Ask your board champion to assemble a board assessment group. Charge this group with assessing the current board's view of philanthropy and best practices and highlighting the gap between where the board is currently and where it wants to be and why. Have the group establish a time frame for addressing these issues, listing resources needed to do so and outlining expected outcomes. This group can consist of a few board members if your board is large, or all board members if your board is small.

"We did this with our board three years ago," says Dellaripa. "Some of the outcomes of our effort included board responsibility documents, board diversity plans and policies, a dashboard for tracking board philanthropy efforts, and board subcommittees to enhance philanthropy. First board members' thoughts changed, and then their behaviors. Our board members are now more satisfied, and feel successful and proud of their efforts, knowing they did this for themselves."

*Aaron Berger, Partner, Alexander Haas (Atlanta, GA):*

Adding a half- or full-day to your board retreat to allow board members to look at their own roles, expectations, effectiveness and satisfaction is a great way to allow your individual board members to suggest specific goals for themselves. Berger says: "This way touchy topics like board giving, board member responsibilities, term limits, conflicts of interest, etc., can be discussed among peers in a constructive way."

*Kayte Connelly, Chief Solutions Officer, Principled Solutions LLC (West Chester, PA):*

According to Connelly, many times boards are stuck because their members do not understand their roles as chief policy makers.

"Policy dictates all money issues — spending money, watching money, raising money," she says. "Executive directors may experience a setback because their board gets mired in muck and can't move on to the issues of money."

Connelly, named 2009 Small Business Philanthropist by the Philadelphia Business Journal, says the task of raising money needs to be approached by the board reasonably, responsibly, and with great regularity:

- **Reasonably** means the board needs to set clear expectations and board members need to commit to them annually.

- **Responsibly** means the board needs to conduct an assessment and provide training for areas where remedial actions are needed to support the board's work.

- **Regularly** means the board needs to use frequent accountability measures throughout the year, in the form of quarterly reports through committee actions, individual actions, etc. "These types of reports can propel the worst of boards forward in their goals," she says.

Sources: Aaron Berger, Partner, Alexander Haas, Atlanta, GA. Phone (404) 525-7575.
E-mail: aaron.berger@fundraisingcounsel.com
Kayte Connelly, Chief Solutions Officer, Principled Solutions LLC, West Chester, PA. Phone (484) 769-2327.
E-mail: Kayte@bestprincipledsolutions.com
Sondra Dellaripa, Vice President, Development & Major Gifts Officer, Eastern Connecticut Health Network, CT Foundation & Philanthropy Consultant, Manchester, CT.
Phone (860) 647-6877. E-mail: sdellaripa@echn.org

*Building Your Board: How to Attract Financially-Capable Board Members and Engage Them in Fund Development.* Edited by Scott C. Stevenson. © 2010 Stevenson, Inc. Published 2010 by Stevenson, Inc.

*To keep board members energized and motivated, take advantage of every opportunity to acknowledge their support and involvement. Celebrate their victories. Publicize their invaluable connection to your organization and its work.*

## Develop a Section of Board Feature Ideas

To what degree are you doing feature stories about both your collective board and individual board members? Don't overlook the benefits of stories related to your organization's top leaders. Articles about those who oversee your organization add another level of credibility to your cause. Plus, readers find such human interest stories to be of interest.

Develop a checklist of board-related story ideas from which to choose for internal and external publications, for news releases to distribute to area news media, and for feature ideas to handfeed news media. Here are some story angles to consider:

- Percentage of board support for your recent capital campaign.
- Collective power of your board: A profile of the positions of influence they hold.
- Ways your board is making a difference for people served by your organization.
- A profile of how one board member's major gift is making a noticeable difference at your organization.
- Examples of how your board has taken a visionary approach in addressing its future.
- How one board member continues to go the extra mile in service.
- Profiles of what attracted board members to your cause.
- A question/answer interview with a board member about a relevant topic with which he/she has expertise.

In addition to bringing valuable visibility to your cause, the publication of these stories will also serve to further cultivate board members' commitment to your organization.

## Include Board Bios on Your Website

There are several reasons why you should publicly affiliate your board members with your organization: they add credibility to your cause; they take on greater ownership of your organization; and they deserve all of the accolades you can give them.

Showcase your board by including brief biographies and photos of each of them on your website. Make them interesting by sharing something of a more personal nature: what they enjoy doing in their spare time, what matters most to them or whom they most admired and why.

### Examples of Nonprofits Showcasing Their Board Members

KVMR, Nevada City, CA
www.kvmr.org/bod/index.html

Cascade Land Conservancy, Seattle, WA
www.cascadeland.org/about-clc/board/board-bios

CPRIT, Austin, TX
www.cprit.state.tx.us/boardbios.html

### Get and Use Board Photos

As part of your effort to build a board of "movers and shakers," get a quality photo of each board member as he/she joins your ranks, even if it means paying for it. Once you've done that, use it.

Using board photos accomplishes two goals: 1) it lets the public see the stature of those associated with and committed to your cause and 2) it serves to further cultivate (and steward) a board member every time it is used.

## Get Board Members Talking With Clever Thank-yous

One way to keep your nonprofit organization on the tips of your board members' tongues is to acknowledge their contributions and service with one-of-a-kind thank-you gifts.

While a thank-you note, polo shirt or photo in your organization's newsletter are kind and genuine ways to express your gratitude, they aren't necessarily unique conversation starters. Find a creative, attention-getting way to say thanks, however, and you will not only leave your board members feeling special, you will give them a reason to tell others about the gesture and, ultimately, your cause.

Think of your thank-you gestures as another way to market your organization.

Such gifts or gestures do not have to be costly. In fact, inexpensive ones usually come across as more clever.

Try one of these suggestions the next time a board member or other volunteer makes a special contribution or goes the extra mile:

❑ **Celebrate a bright idea.** If someone comes up with a terrific idea at a board meeting, say thanks at the next meeting with a light bulb and a colorful tag that reads:

"Thanks for the bright idea!" Environmentally conscious nonprofit organizations should, of course, give an energy-efficient bulb.

❑ **Say thanks with a sweet gesture.** A person who offered to help in a sticky situation — like stepping in to volunteer at an event that is short-staffed — would be delighted to receive a pack of LifeSavers candies or bottle of locally produced honey or maple syrup, also with a colorful beribboned tag saying: "Thanks for helping us out of a sticky situation!"

❑ **Let the label tell the value.** A significant fundraising effort or major contribution can be acknowledged with a poster board covered in 100 Grand candy bars that spell "THANKS!" and a note that reads: "Your fundraising skills are worth this much and more!"

❑ **Offer a small token.** No matter what the contribution, a fitting token of appreciation would be an actual token! Bus or subway tokens are appreciated by anyone who takes mass transit (or, again, is on the board of an environmentally conscious organization).

## Publicizing Board Donations

When it comes to board donations, how to handle the publicity of a gift can sometimes be a bit tricky.

Several trustees on the board at Case Western University (Cleveland, OH) gave over $6 million to their school. The trustees knew that publicizing the gift could benefit Case Western's fundraising efforts, but some of them preferred to remain anonymous. For the occasion, the Case University trustees and development team worked together to create a specialized leadership story to communicate the trustee gift as a symbol of their strength as an organization overall, rather than focusing on the generosity of individuals.

Several important fundraising issues were brought up when the trustees and development team determined how to handle the publicity for the gift. Those ideas included:

• **Board gifts speak well of your organization.** Trustee gifts instill confidence in an organization, and the announcement of such gifts should be used as an opportunity to encourage other trustees to give. In their announcement, Case Western University reiterated past instances of board giving, reminding their community that since fiscal year 2008-09, the university had earned $108 million in total fundraising, much of which came after major trustee gift announcements.

• **Tailor gift response to your donor's needs.** Remember that gift publicity is an important form of stewardship,

as well as publicity. Hold a special meeting with your donor to determine how your organization can recognize them in such a way that highlights the area in which they're giving, in a way that is appropriate and meaningful for them.

• **Create continuity.** With such a donor-specific approach, it is important to be diligent about tracking your project's progress. Amy Raufman, head of development communications at Case Western Reserve University, and Lara Kalafatis, vice president of university relations at Case Western Reserve University, emphasize the importance of archiving your work with donors, even after the donation is closed. "The donor needs to see relationship with your institution as unified," Kalafatis says. One way to achieve this unification is to integrate your development and communication teams. This allows a streamlined full-service experience for the donor, wherein their needs are more likely to be fully met. At Case Western Reserve University, they created a director of donor communications position, for the exclusive purpose of managing communications with donors and media.

*Sources: Amy Raufman, Head of Development Communications, and Lara Kalafatis, Vice President of University Relations at Case Western Reserve University, Cleveland, OH. Phone (216) 368-0547. E-mail: aer25@case.edu (Raufman). Website: www.case.edu*

*Building Your Board: How to Attract Financially-Capable Board Members and Engage Them in Fund Development.* Edited by Scott C. Stevenson.
© 2010 Stevenson, Inc. Published 2010 by Stevenson, Inc.

## KEEP 'RETIRED' BOARD MEMBERS ENGAGED

*Board term limits are good. They help to ensure ongoing vitality of new board members becoming involved as others leave the board. But just because someone's term on your board has ended doesn't mean the relationship needs to conclude as well. Retiring board members need to know their relationship is ongoing. They may not regularly attend board meetings anymore, but they still have a role to play. You still want and need their involvement as much as ever. Take steps to ensure they stay connected with your organization in very meaningful ways.*

### Stay Connected With Former Board Members

Developing strong relationships with current board members is key to staying connected with them after they retire.

"There is a greater chance of keeping former board members engaged if they were developed and cultivated during their tenure on the board," says Diane Dean, principal, The Dean Consulting Group in the greater New York City area. "There is a unique advantage to having informed insight regarding board members' interests, talents, skills and reasons for committing to the organization on a volunteer leadership level."

Tools to help develop and sustain relationships could include personal questionnaires, self-assessments and committee evaluations, as well as ice-breaker activities during orientations and board retreats. Forming a board development committee charged with recruitment, engagement and development of board members is another useful strategy.

"The best board strategies, the ones that get results that can be tracked to prove success, are those that are incorporated as programs with written procedures and a clear goal of what success looks like," says Paul Nazareth, Manager of Planned and Personal Giving at the Catholic Archdiocese of Toronto.

A well-crafted communications plan should also include a formal recognition process for people coming on and off the board.

"One innovative idea I've seen is an organization that will add a 'recommendation' to a board member's LinkedIn profile if he or she fulfills the top five criteria of an 'excellent board' (commitment to the board, volunteer in programs, advocate in the community, network for the organization, make a leadership or planned gift)," Nazareth says.

One way to engage retiring board members that many organizations overlook is to actually ask what kind of involvement they would like to have going forward. Some board members are ready for a well-deserved rest after years of service. Others are still eager to contribute their time and talents. The executive director and/or board president should initiate a conversation with board members as their terms near an end. Ask what level of involvement they would like and whether that involvement would be immediately after the end of their board service or a couple years down the road.

> ### Give 'Retired' Board Members Options
>
> Potential roles for former board members could include:
>
> - Serving as mentors to new board members.
> - Membership in or leadership of special task forces/fundraising campaigns of a limited duration.
> - Membership in an honorary advisory committee.
> - Ex-official membership in select committees.

*Sources: Diane D. Dean, principal, The Dean Consulting Group, Rutherford, NJ. Phone (800) 686-1975
E-mail: ddean@thedeanconsultinggroup.com
Website: http://www.thedeanconsultinggroup.com
Paul Nazareth, manger, Planned and Personal Giving at Catholic Archdiocese of Toronto, Toronto, Ontario, Canada.
Phone (416) 934-3411. E-mail: pnazareth@archtoronto.org
Website: www.archtoronto.org*

### Keep Retiring Board Members In the Fold

Here's the usual pattern: You discover someone with financial capability, take steps to involve him/her in the life of your organization — quite often serving on a committee or advisory council — and then eventually move the individual to your board of directors (or trustees) to serve out as many terms as is possible before the person is retired.

But then what? Is that it?

It doesn't have to be. Rather than putting board members out to pasture, consider reversing the process. Once a board member retires, offer him/her the opportunity to stay connected with your organization by rejoining one of your committees or advisory groups again. The board member will be much more in tune with what he/she finds most fulfilling about your organization and can select a new point of involvement that will be mutually rewarding.

## Pros and Cons of Board Term Limits

Are you thinking about revamping your board's term limits? Consider these pros and cons of term limits:

*Pros* —

- Fresh blood and perspectives will rejuvenate a stale board.
- Turnover keeps a board in touch with the altering needs of its community.
- Convenient way to let ineffective members go without confrontation.
- Fatigue, boredom and loss of commitment prevention.
- Frequent open slots allow for more effective, motivated and willing people to serve.

*Cons* —

- Board may lose organizational memory.
- Constant need for education, team building and orientation of the organization's history and mission.
- An organization may lose some of its best people — passionate, active members.
- Prevents members from having a deeper understanding of the organization.
- Continually recruiting committed people may be difficult.

## Give Former Board Members Status, Involvement Avenues

Unless your organization is one of those that keeps the same board members term after term — and that would be a big mistake — you should see an orderly turnover among this group of individuals. So what becomes of these capable individuals when they are "put out to pasture?" Do they simply fade away into your vast pool of constituents?

Take special measures regarding this group of former policy makers. Give them ongoing status by establishing an emeritus trustee society or club. Whenever you host a social function for current board members, consider including your emeritus board members and their spouses as well. Keep them up-to-date on matters of interest. Look for special ways of involving them as volunteers.

These unique individuals — many of whom may have made generous gifts to your organization — deserve exclusive cultivation and stewardship measures.

## Don't Overlook the Potential of Past Board Members

When you're new to a development position there are standard actions to take to get up to speed: get to know the staff; become familiar with goals, objectives and action plans; meet current board members and top donors, and more.

Researching past board members is another move you might want to take. Often board members contribute while they are active but once their terms are finished, the financial support wanes (or stops all together). Sometimes that end to support is the result of insufficient attention from development officials.

Become familiar with those who have served as board members in the past. Take the time to introduce yourself to them. Become familiar with their individual connections to your new organization. Chances are you will reestablish some important ties that would have otherwise never been rekindled.

## Host a Reception for All Past Board Members

Many nonprofits give former board members emeritus status as a way to keep them involved after their terms end. Unfortunately, far more nonprofits do little or nothing to maintain that relationship with former board members.

If your nonprofit has let relationships with former board members slide, why not coordinate an event geared just for them? Here's how you might do that:

1. Pull together a committee made up of current and former board members, and charge them with coordinating a board appreciation event.
2. Suggest that the committee schedule an event with some drawing card appeal — perhaps at an exquisite home that visitors would love to visit.
3. In addition to plenty of social time, incorporate a brief program that brings past board members up to speed on your nonprofit's current happenings. In fact, you might want to ask these former board members if they would like the group to continue on a more formal basis, perhaps meeting twice a year or quarterly.

If the group of former board members agrees to move forward in a more official capacity, you may want to involve them in any number of fund development activities.